ATLAS OF
TOWN PLANS

Reprinted July 1996
Reprinted April 1996
Reprinted October 1995
3rd edition July 1995
2nd edition April 1994
Reprinted June 1994
Reprinted November 1994
Reprinted March 1995
Reprinted September 1995
1st edition April 1992

**This edition is exclusive to WHSmith Ltd,
Greenbridge Road, Swindon, SN3 3LD**

Published by AA Publishing (a trading name of Automobile Association
Developments Limited, whose registered office is Norfolk House, Priestley
Road, Basingstoke, Hampshire RG24 9NY. Registered number 1878835).

ISBN 0 7495 1470 1

Mapping produced by the Cartographic Department of The Automobile
Association. This atlas has been compiled and produced from the
Automaps database utilising electronic and computer technology.

Printed by BPC Waterlow Ltd, Dunstable.

(iii)

CONTENTS

Town plan location map and map symbols
(iii)

Town Plans
2-123

Mileage Chart
124

Town Plans

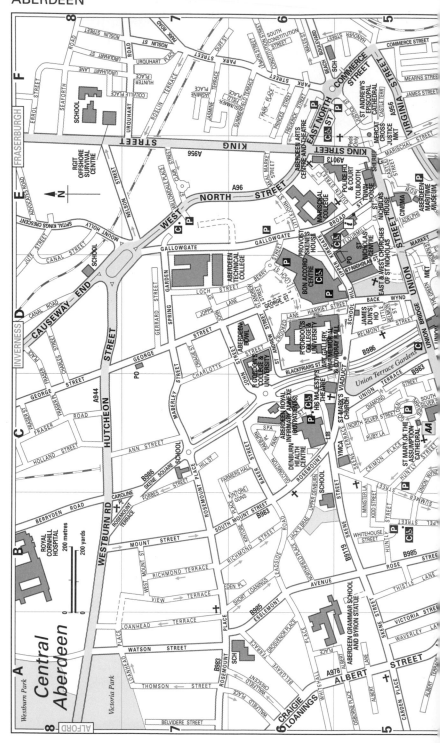

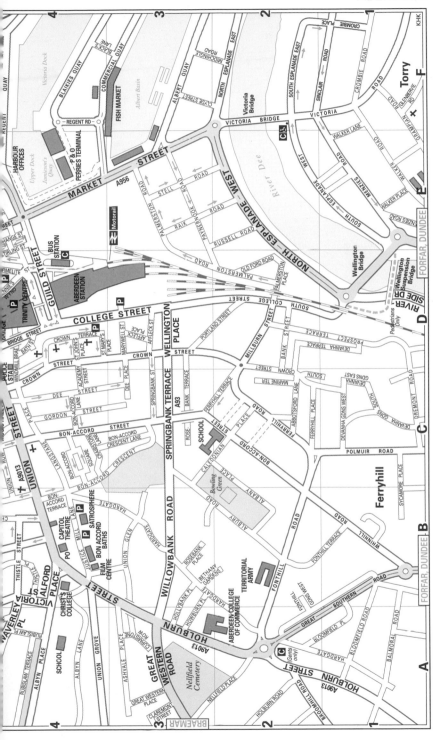

ABERYSTWYTH ANDOVER

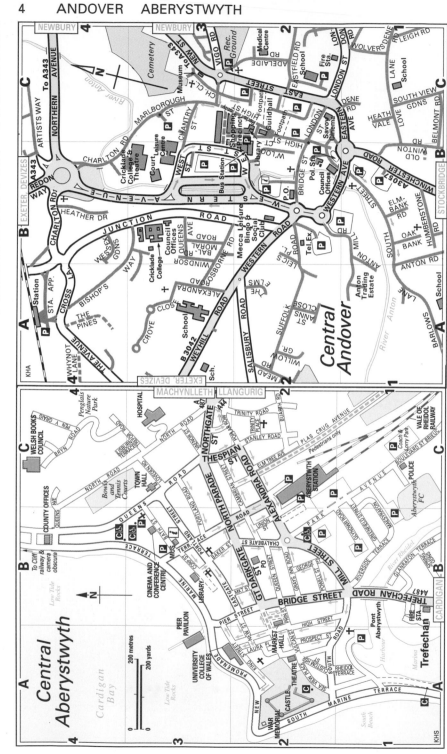

Central Andover

Central Aberystwyth

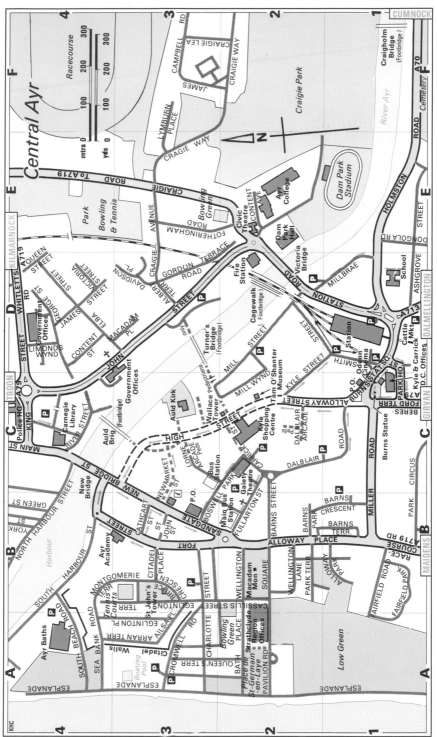

AYR

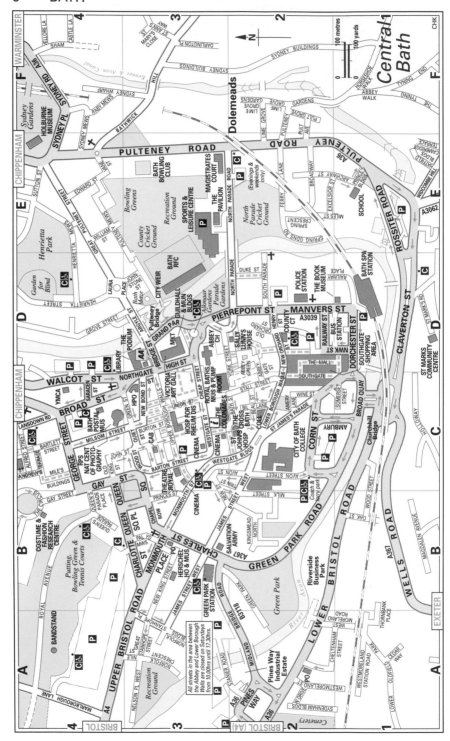

BLACKPOOL

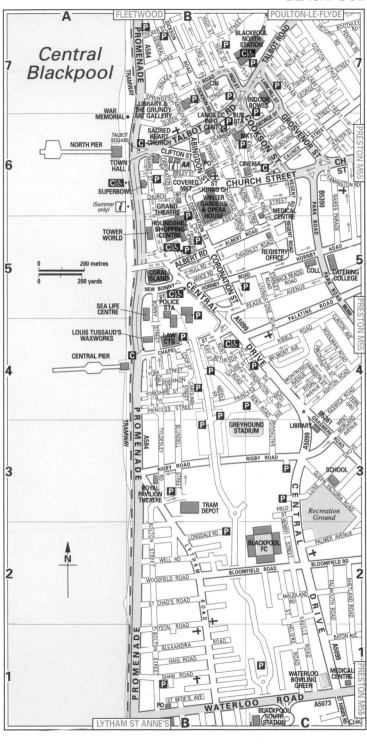

Central Blackpool

FLEETWOOD

POULTON-LE-FLYDE

PRESTON M55

PRESTON M55

PRESTON M55

WAR MEMORIAL

NORTH PIER

TALBOT SQUARE

TOWN HALL

LIBRARY & THE GRUNDY ART GALLERY

SACRED HEART CHURCH

COVERED MKT

SUPERBOWL

(Summer only)

GRAND THEATRE

TOWER WORLD

HOUNDSHILL SHOPPING CENTRE

CORAL ISLAND

SEA LIFE CENTRE

LOUIS TUSSAUD'S WAXWORKS

CENTRAL PIER

POLICE STA

LAW CTS

WINTER GARDENS & OPERA HOUSE

MEDICAL CENTRE

REGISTRY OFFICE

COLL

CATERING COLLEGE

BLACKPOOL NORTH STATION

INDOOR BOWLS

LANOS CC INFO CENTRE

BUS STA

MKT

CINEMA

ST JOHNS CH

LIBRARY

GREYHOUND STADIUM

SCHOOL

ROYAL PAVILION THEATRE

TRAM DEPOT

Recreation Ground

BLACKPOOL FC

MAUDLAND RD

MEDICAL CENTRE

WATERLOO BOWLING GREEN

BLACKPOOL SOUTH STATION

LYTHAM ST ANNE'S

PROMENADE

TRAMWAY

0   200 metres

0   200 yards

N

BIRMINGHAM

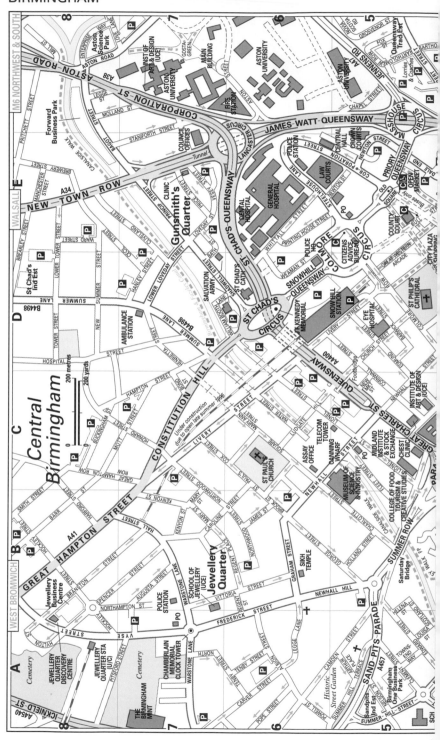

BIRMINGHAM

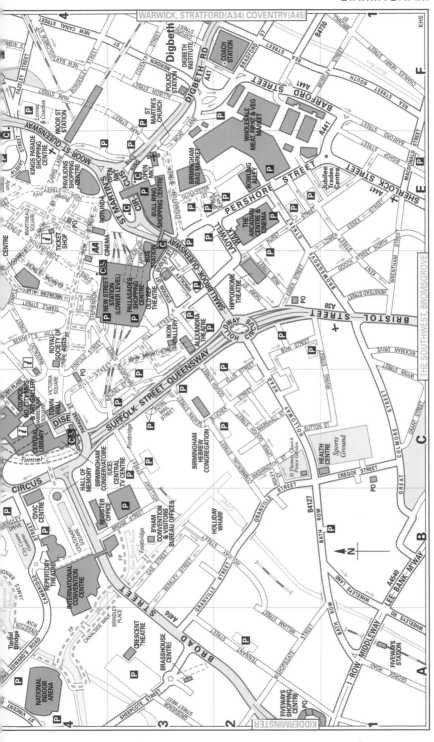

BOLTON

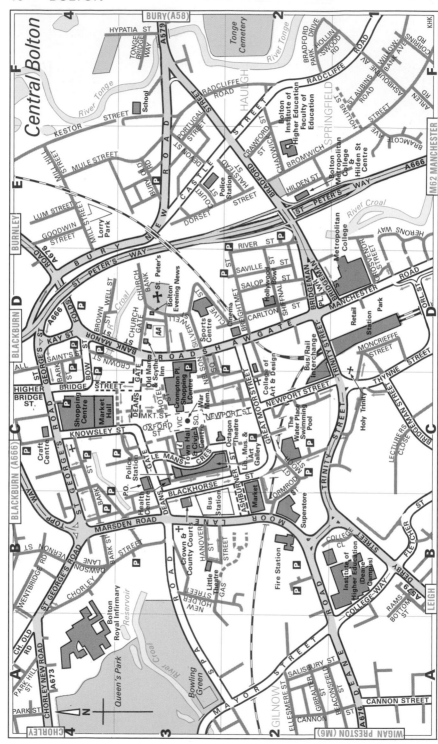

Central Bolton

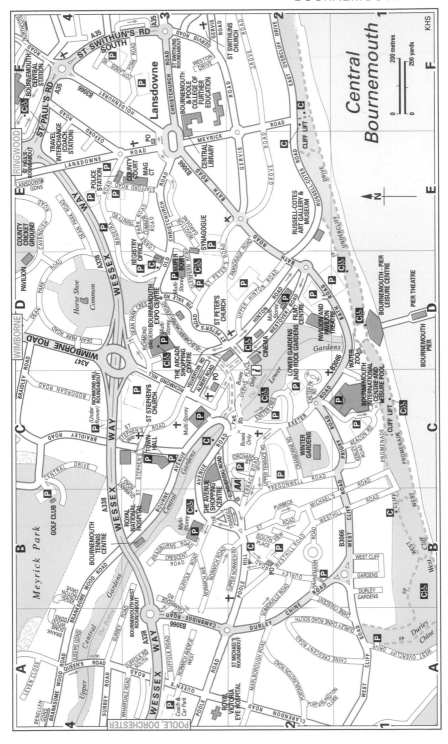

BOURNEMOUTH

BRISTOL

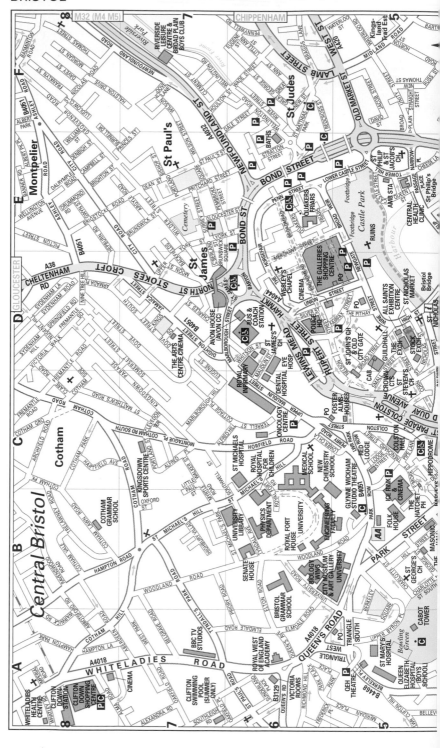

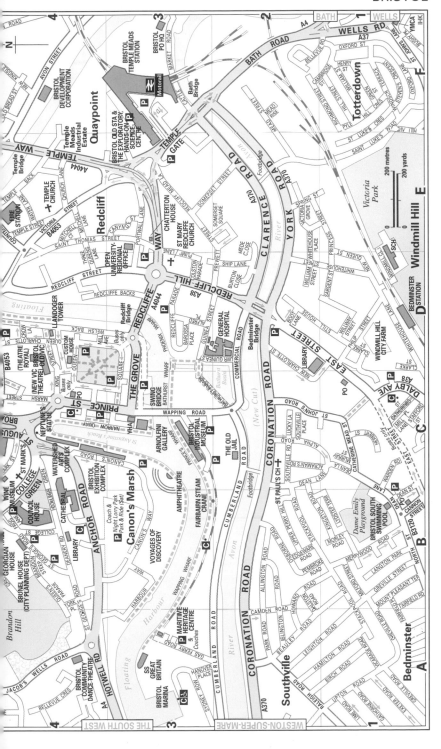

BRISTOL

BRADFORD

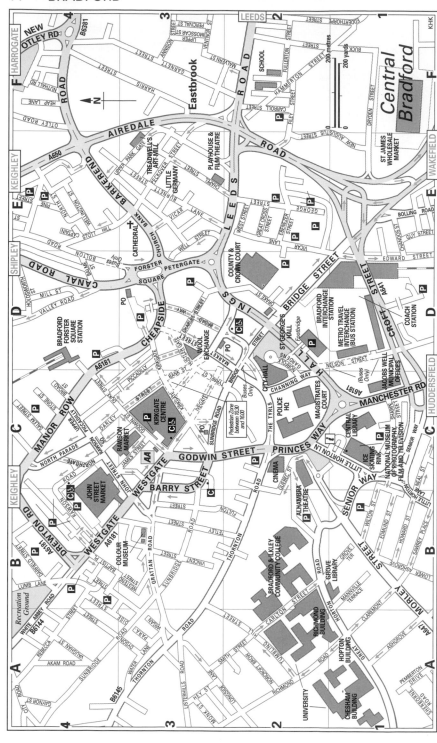

BRIGHTON

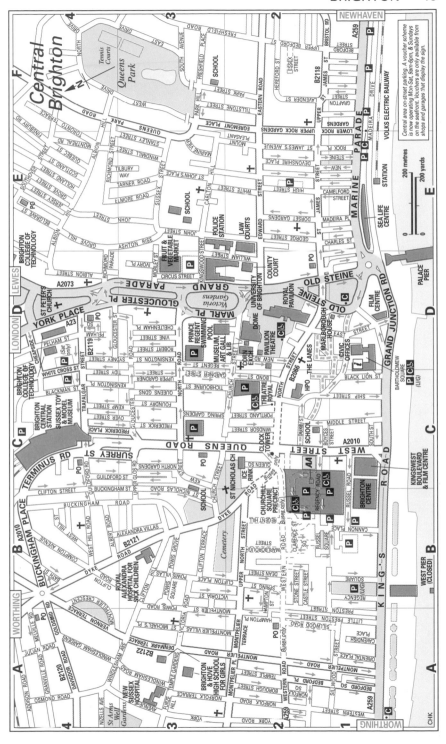

Central area on-street parking. A voucher scheme is now operating Mon–Sat, 9am–6pm, & Sundays on the seafront. Vouchers are only available from shops and garages that display the sign.

VOLKS ELECTRIC RAILWAY

200 metres
200 yards

NEWHAVEN

WORTHING

LEWES

LONDON

WORTHING

CHK

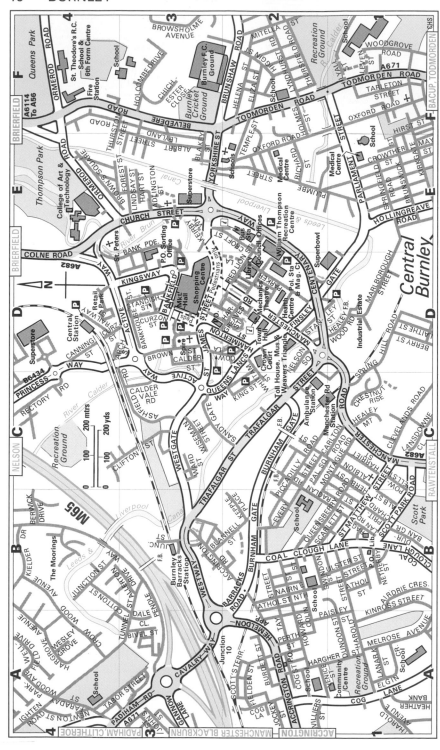

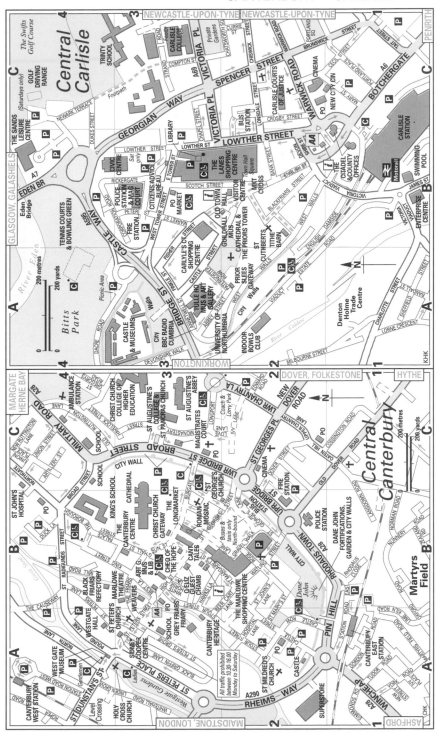

CAMBRIDGE

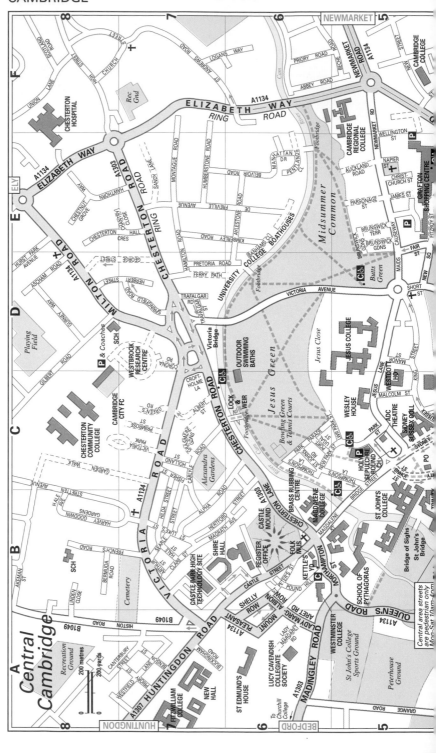

CAMBRIDGE

CARDIFF

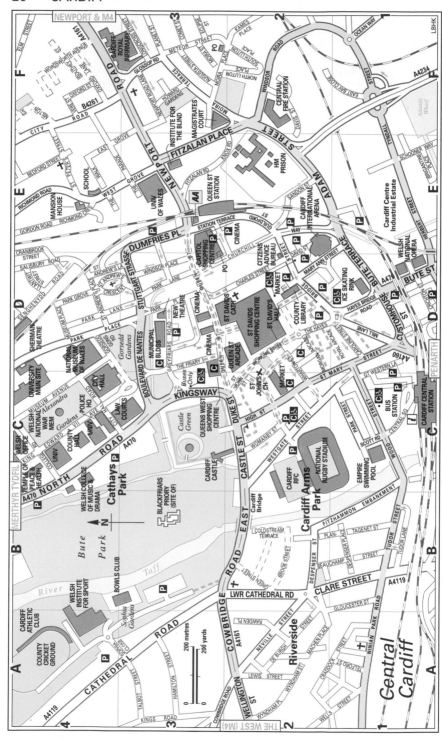

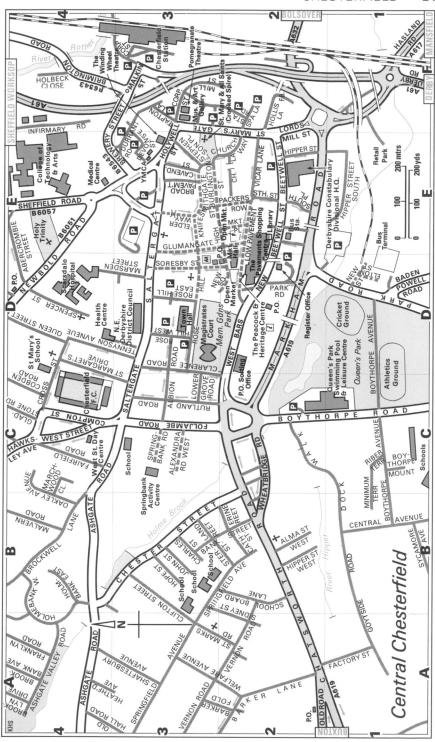

CHESTERFIELD

Central Chesterfield

CHELMSFORD

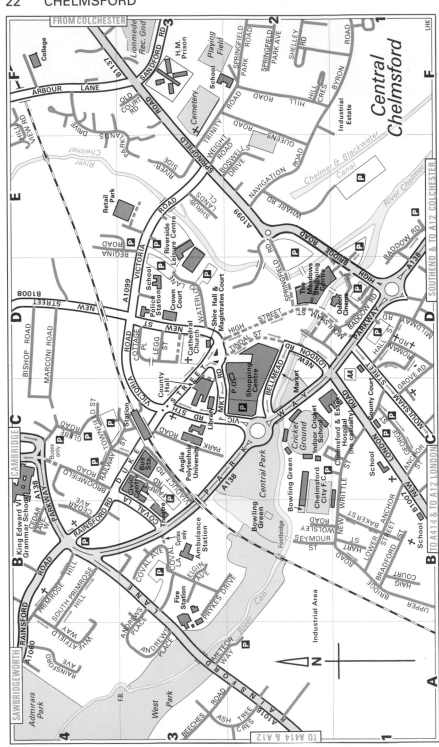

Central Chelmsford

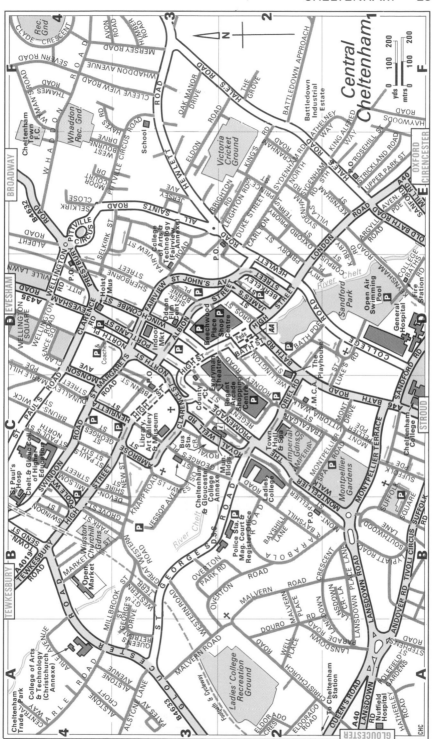

CHELTENHAM

CHESTER

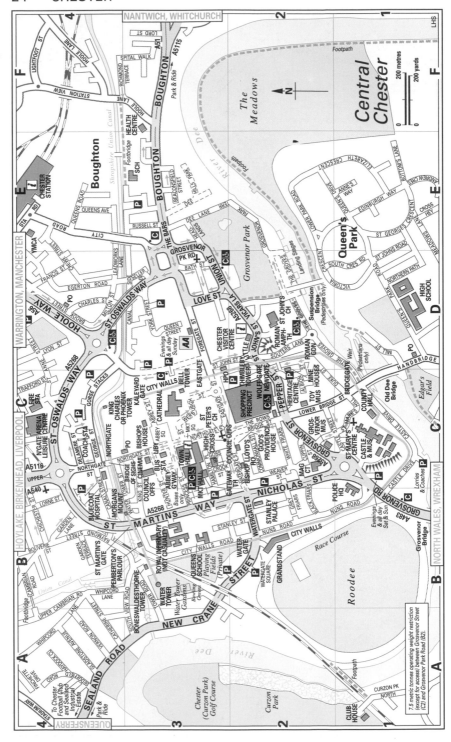

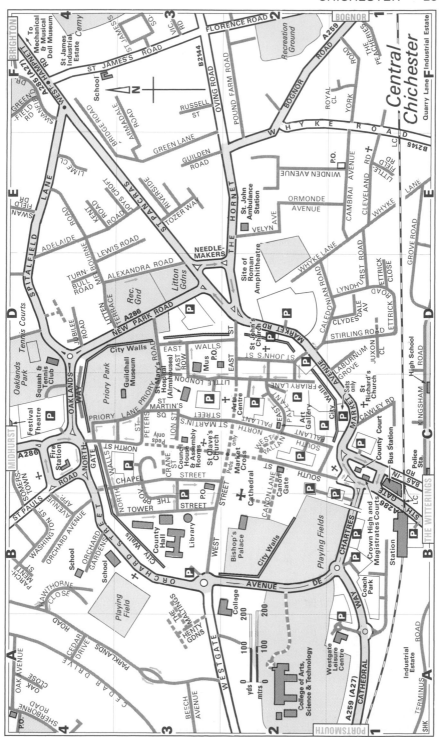

CHICHESTER

Central Chichester

COLCHESTER

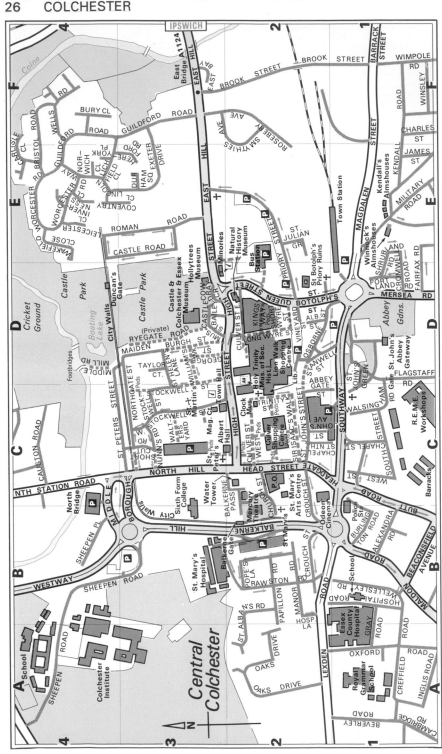

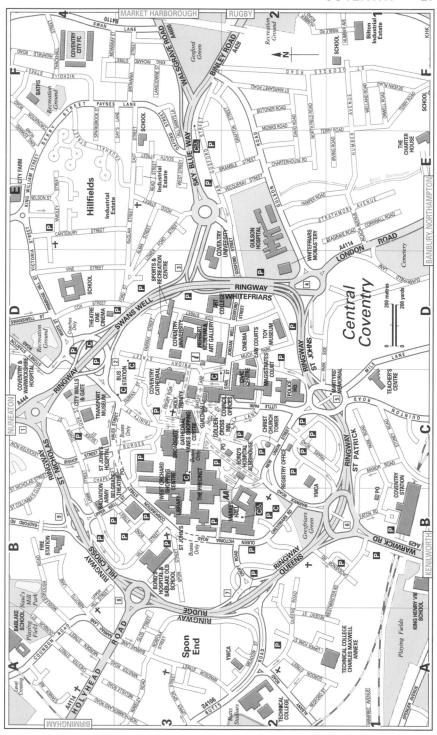

COVENTRY

DARLINGTON

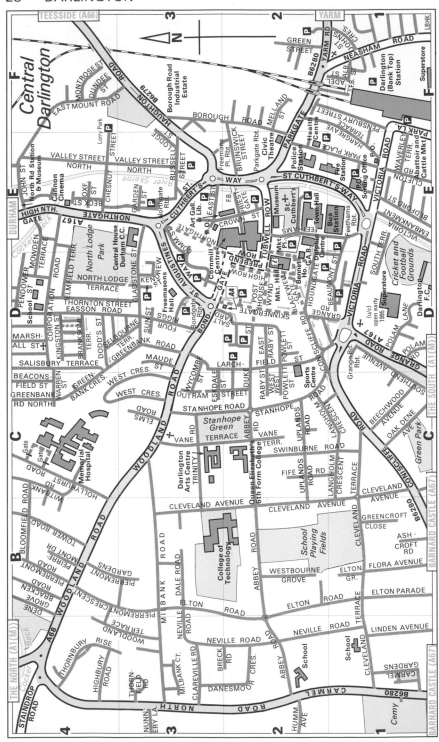

DOVER

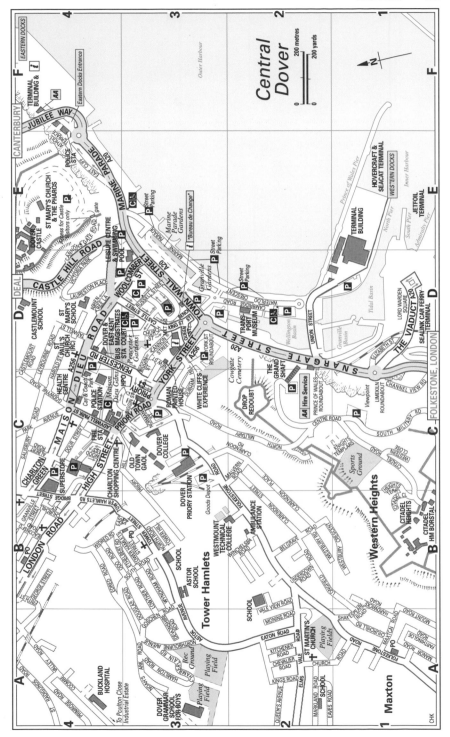

Central Dover

200 metres
200 yards

EASTERN DOCKS

Eastern Docks Entrance

TERMINAL BUILDING & AA

CANTERBURY

JUBILEE WAY

POLICE STA

St Martin Price Ho

ST MARY'S CHURCH & THE PHAROS

DOVER CASTLE

CASTLE HILL ROAD

DEAL

CASTLEMOUNT SCHOOL

CASTLEMOUNT ROAD

MAISON DIEU ROAD

MARINE PARADE

M20

FAST CAFÉ

Access for Castle visitors only

LAUREAUN PLACE

ST MARY'S SCHOOL

ST JAMES' CHURCH (REMAINS)

DOVER & EAST KENT MAGISTRATES' CTS

BUS STA

PREESTER'S Gardens

HEALTH CENTRE

CARS

Maison Dieu

Car & Coach Park

POLICE STATION

PRIORY ROAD

FIRE STA

Dover Gdns

Outer Harbour

Marine Parade Gardens

"Bureau de Change"

Street Parking

WOOLCOMBER ST

Street Parking

Street Parking

LEISURE CENTRE & SWIMMING POOL

TOWN WALL STREET

CASTLE STREET

RUSSELL STREET

CANNON STREET

CHURCH ST

MARKET SQ

KING ST

QUEEN ST

YORK STREET

A20

A256

A256

Granville Gardens

Waterloo Crescent

CAMBRIDGE ROAD

UNION STREET

Wellington Basin

Granville Basin

TRANSPORT MUSEUM

CARS

Prince of Wales Pier

North Pier

TERMINAL BUILDING

Tidal Basin

HOVERCRAFT & SEACAT TERMINAL

WESTERN DOCKS

Inner Harbour

JETFOIL TERMINAL

South Pier

Admiralty Pier

LORD WARDEN SQUARE

SEALINK CAR FERRY TERMINAL

THE VIADUCT

ELIZABETH ST

CHANNEL VIEW RD

LIMEKILN ROUNDABOUT

Viewpoint

FOLKESTONE, LONDON

Compate Cemetery

YORK ST ROUNDABOUT

ROMAN PAINTED HOUSE

WHITE CLIFFS EXPERIENCE

DROP REDOUBT

THE GRAND SHAFT

AA Hire Service

PRINCE OF WALES ROUNDABOUT

CENTRE ROAD

SOUTH MILITARY RD

NORTH MILITARY ROAD

MILITARY ROAD

WESTERN ROAD

KNIGHTS TEMPLARS

Sports Ground

CITADEL HEIGHTS

CITADEL

HM BORSTAL

Western Heights

CHARLTON GREEN

SUPERSTORE

HIGH STREET

CHARLTON SHOPPING CENTRE

OLD TOWN GAOL

DOVER COLLEGE

DOVER PRIORY STATION

Goods Depot

WESTMOUNT TECHNICAL COLLEGE

AMBULANCE STATION

BRIDGE STREET

LONDON ROAD

PO

ASTOR SCHOOL

SCHOOL

Tower Hamlets

CLARENDON STREET

LAUREL PLACE

MINCHES RD

BELGRAVE ROAD

SCHOOL

VALE VIEW ROAD

MONINS ROAD

EATON ROAD

ST MARTIN'S CHURCH

Playing Fields

KITCHENER ROAD

CHEVALIER ROAD

KINGS ROAD

VALE ROAD

CHURCH ROAD

QUEEN'S AVENUE

ELMS

MARKLAND ROAD

EAVES ROAD

SCHOOL

FOLKESTONE ROAD

PO

MANOR ROAD

MATHILDE ROAD

MAYFIELD AVE

SHAKESPEARE ROAD

HARMONSE ROAD

CHURCHILL RD

MOUNT ROAD

Maxton

BUCKLAND HOSPITAL

DOVER GRAMMAR SCHOOL FOR BOYS

To Poulton Close Industrial Estate

Playing Field

Rec Ground

Playing Field

CHK

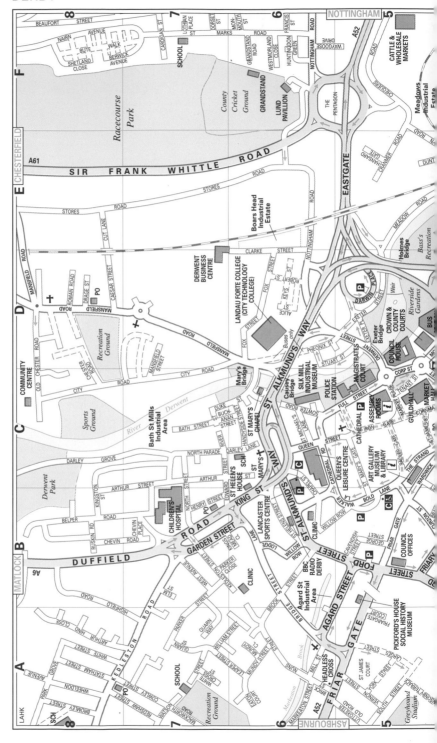

DERBY

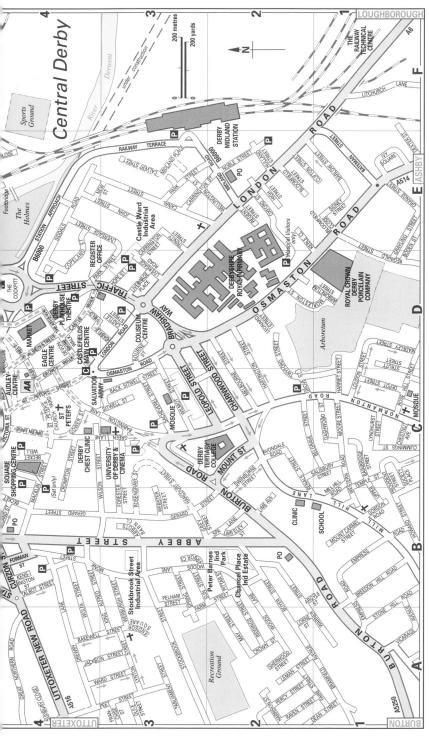

Central Derby

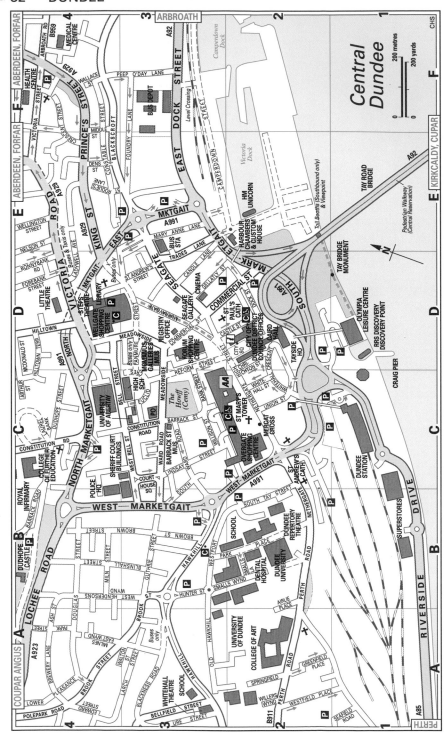

DUNDEE

Central Dundee

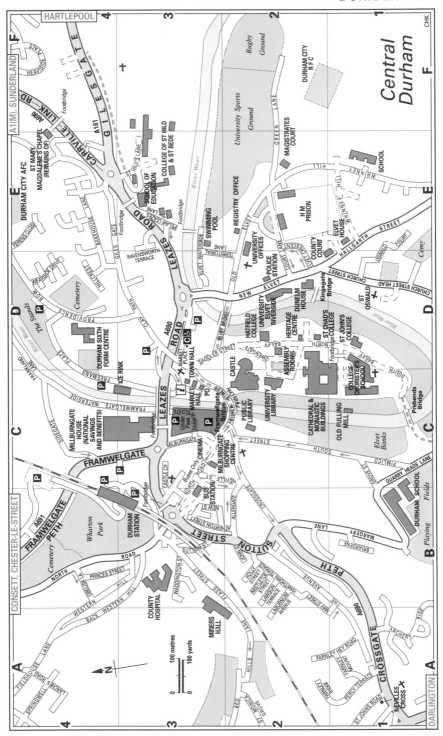

DURHAM

Central Durham

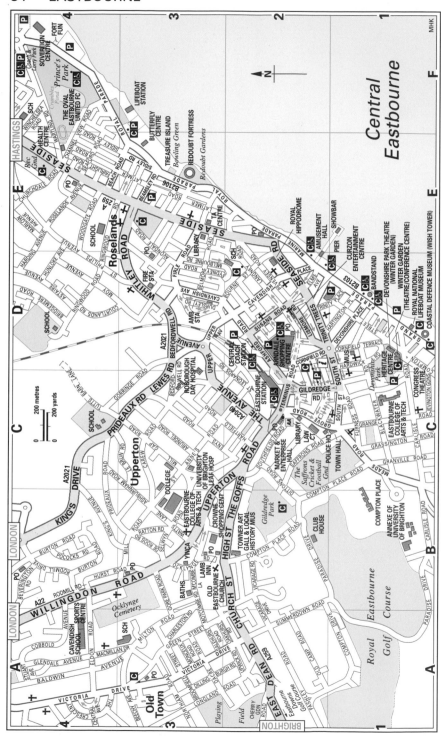

Central Eastbourne

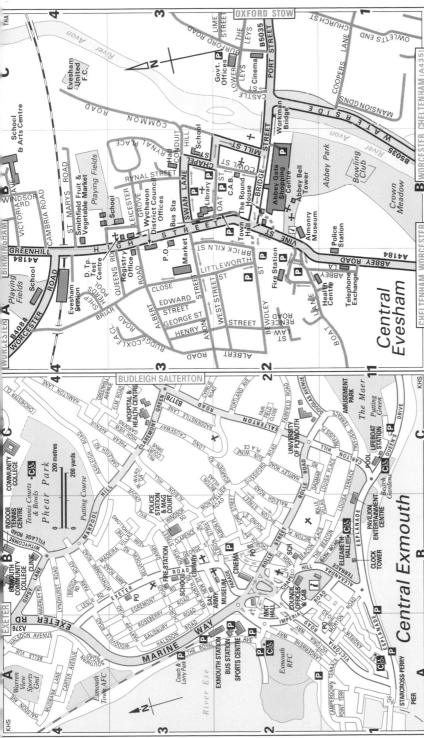

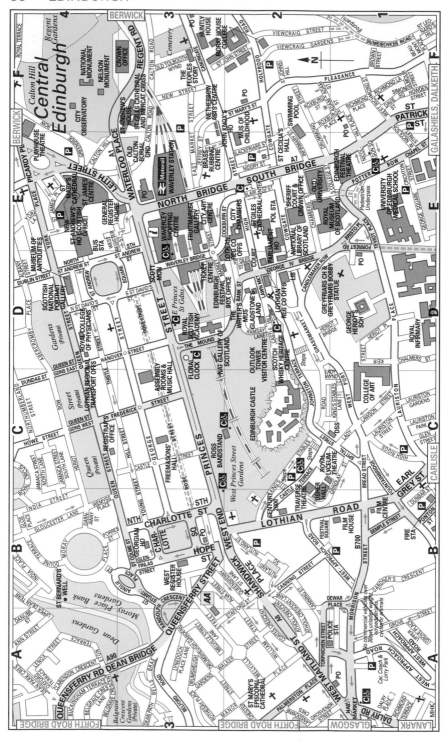

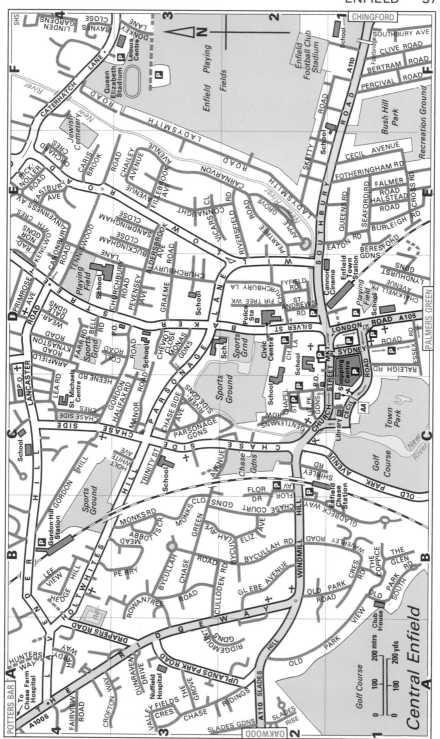

ENFIELD

Central Enfield

EXETER

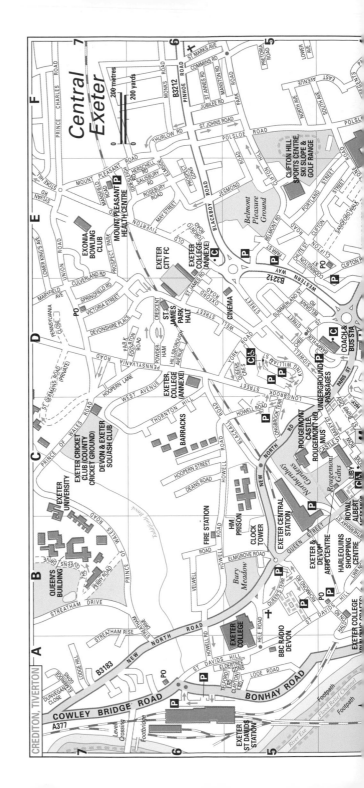

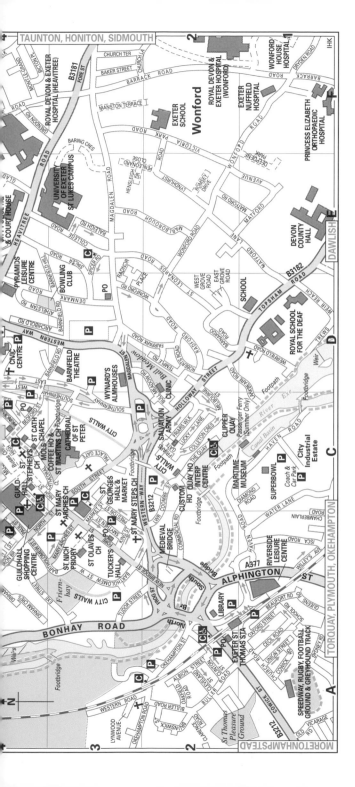

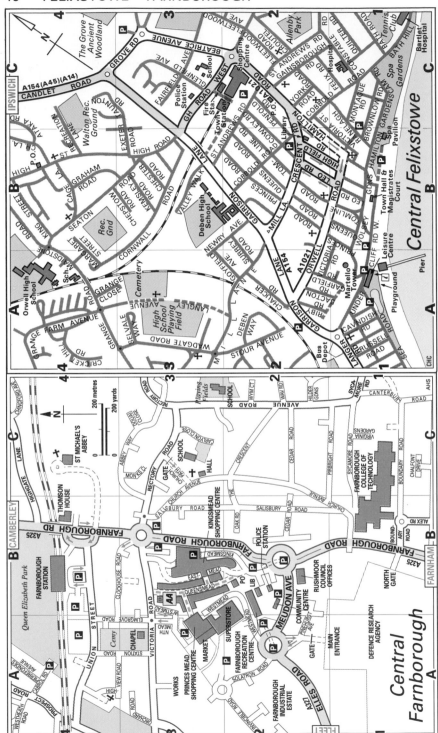

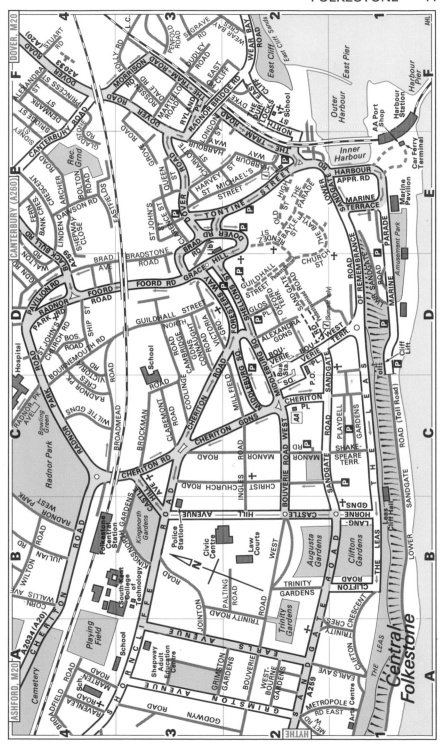

FOLKESTONE

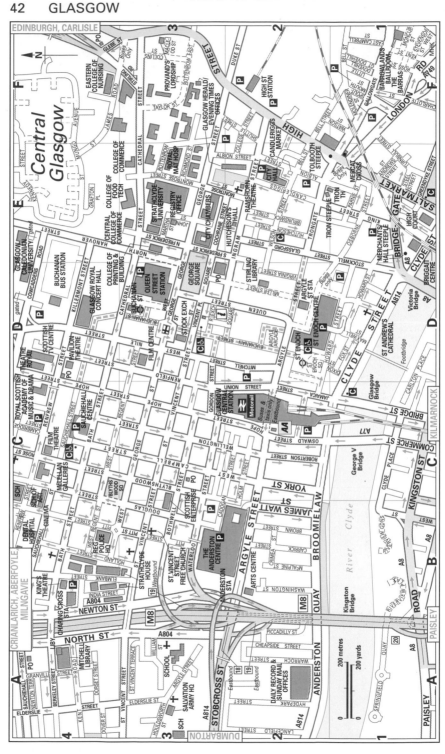

GLOUCESTER

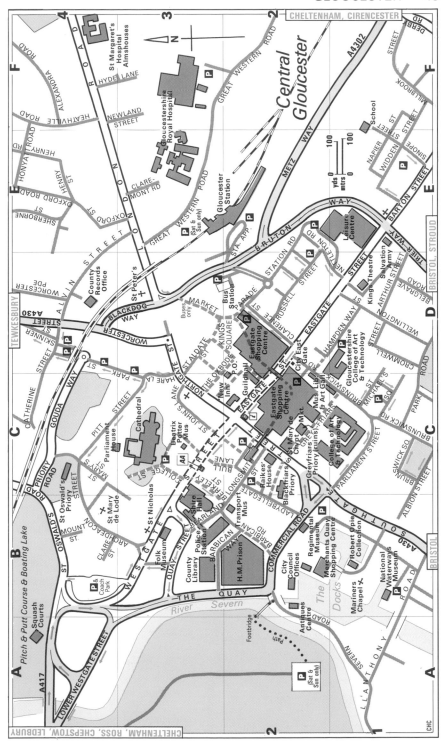

Central Gloucester

CHELTENHAM, ROSS, CHEPSTOW, LEDBURY

BRISTOL, STROUD

BRISTOL

TEWKESBURY

St Margaret's Hospital Almshouses
Gloucestershire Royal Hospital
Gloucester Station
County Records Office
St Peter's
Bus Station
Eastgate Shopping Centre
City East Gate
Leisure Centre
King's Theatre
Salvation Army
Gloucestershire College of Art & Technology
School
New Inn
Guildhall
Mus.Lib. & Art Gall
Eastgate Shopping Centre
St Mary de Crypt
College of Art & Technology
Greyfriars Priory (ruins)
St Michael's
Beatrix Potter Mus
Cathedral
Parliament House
Raikes House
Black Friars Priory
Folk Museum
St Oswald's Priory
St Mary de Lode
St Nicholas
Shire Hall
Police Station
Transport Mus
County Library
City Council Offices
Regimental Museum
H.M.Prison
Merchants Quay Shopping Centre
Robert Opie Collection
Mariners Chapel
National Waterways Museum
Antiques Centre
The Docks
River Severn
Footbridge
Pitch & Putt Course & Boating Lake
Squash Courts
Coach Park

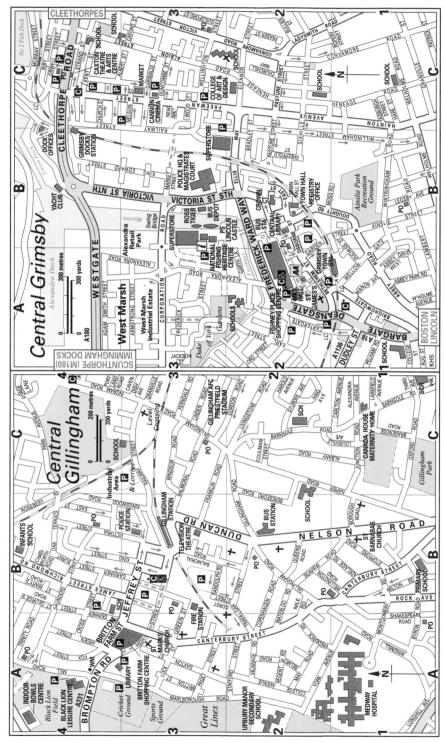

GRIMSBY

GILLINGHAM

Central Grimsby

Central Gillingham

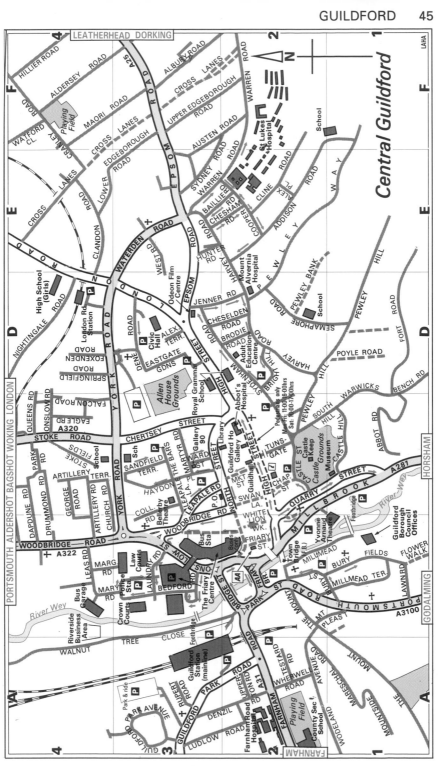

GUILDFORD

Central Guildford

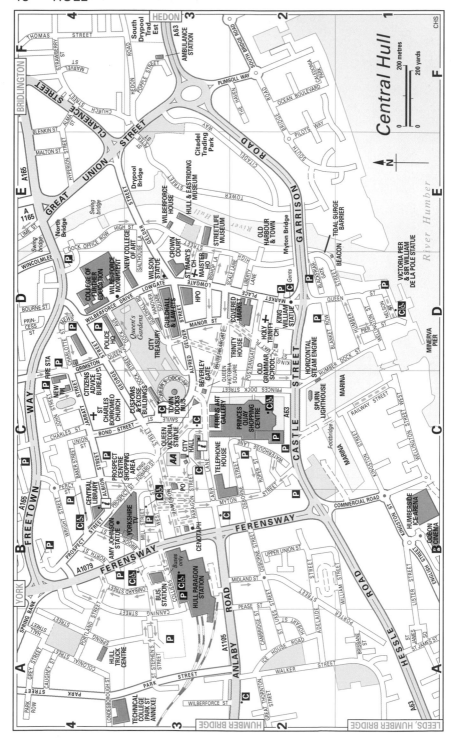

HULL

Central Hull

HOLYHEAD   INVERNESS

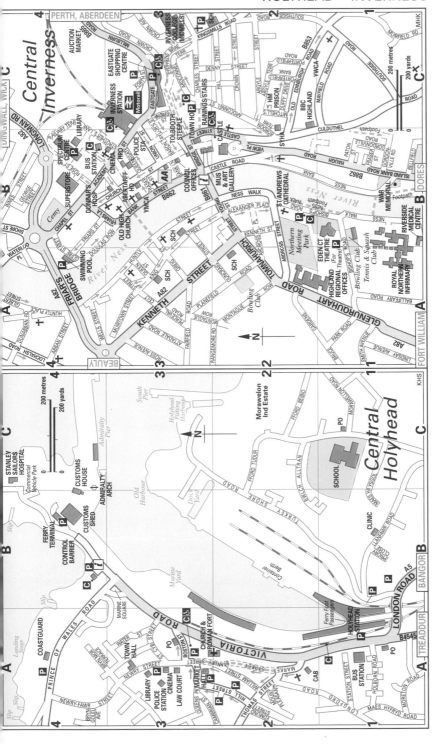

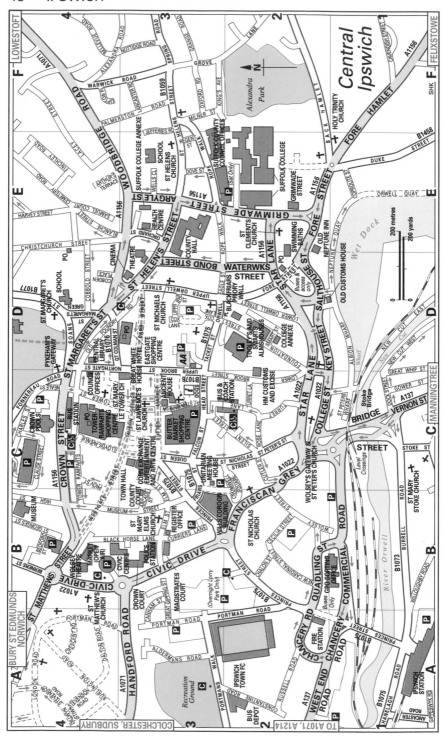

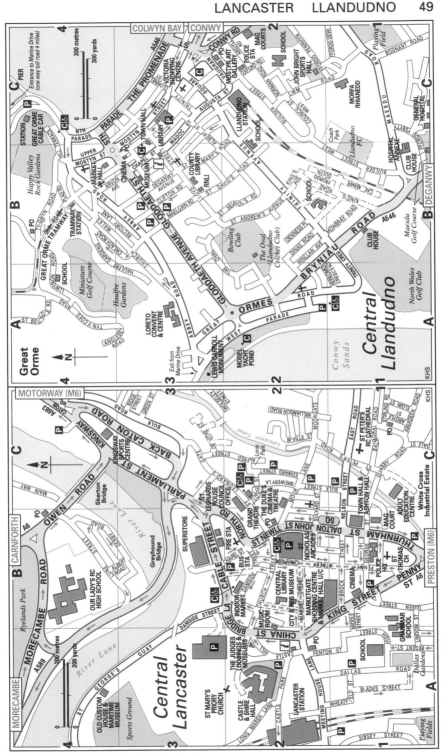

LANCASTER LLANDUDNO

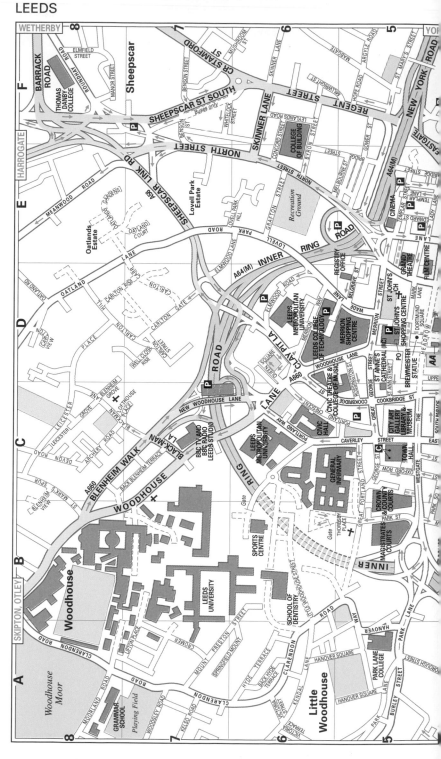

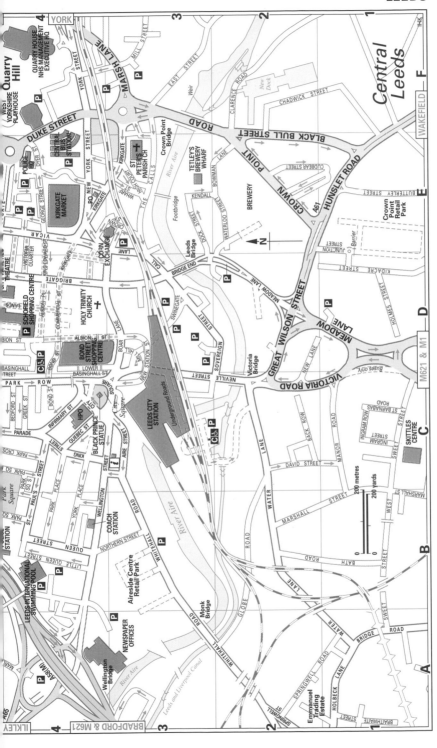

LEEDS

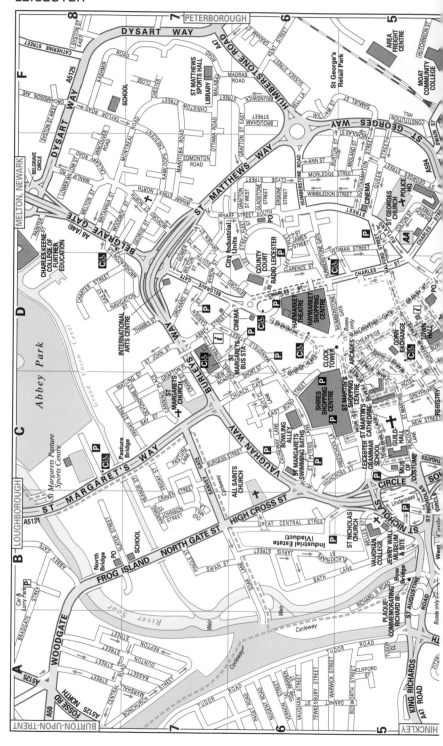

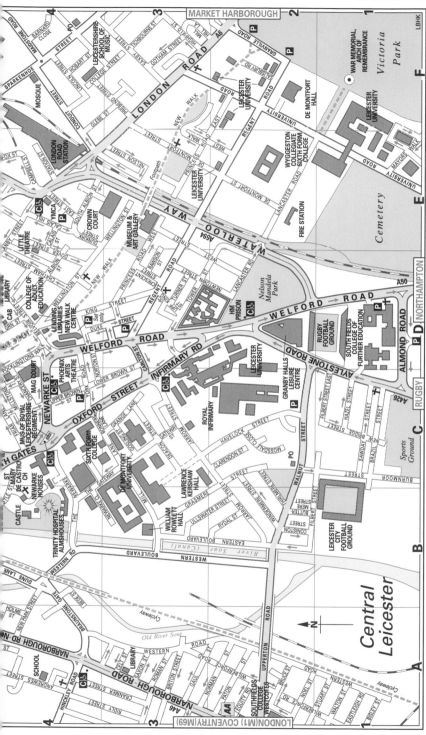

LEICESTER

LINCOLN

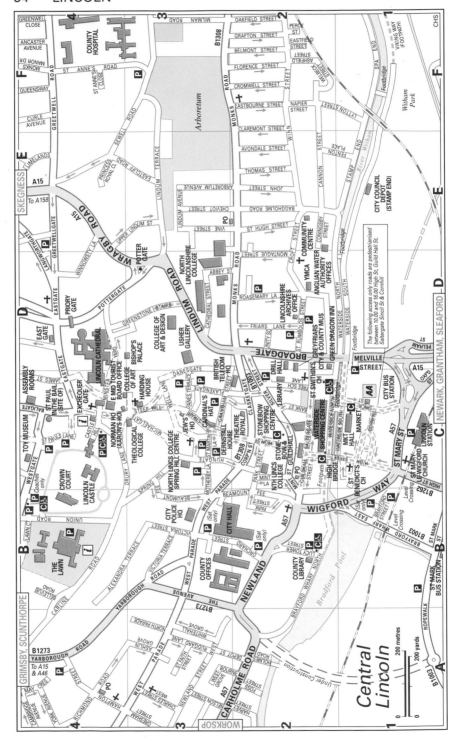

Central Lincoln

LUTON

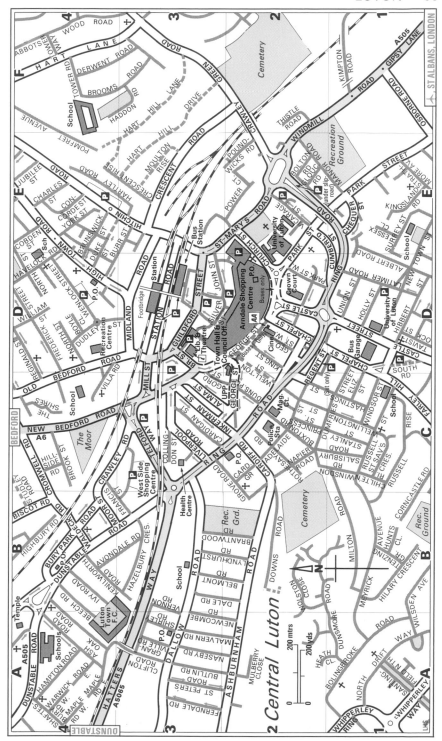

2 Central Luton

LIVERPOOL

LIVERPOOL

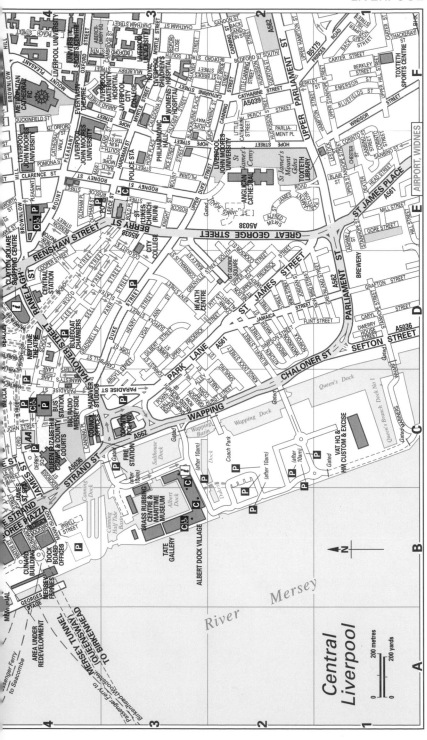

Central Liverpool

0 200 metres
0 200 yards

LONDON

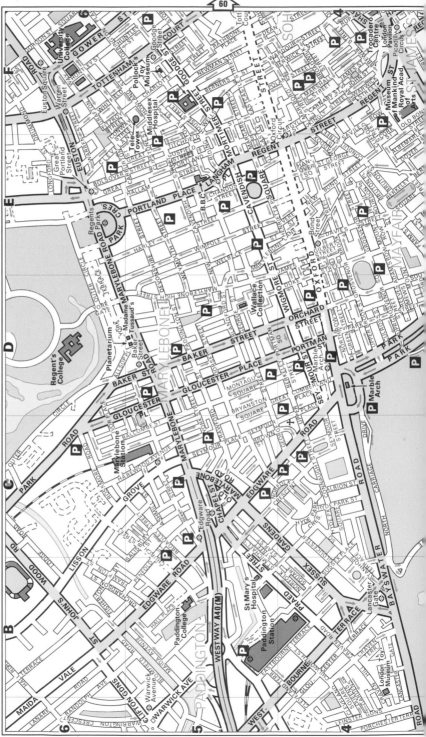

LONDON

61

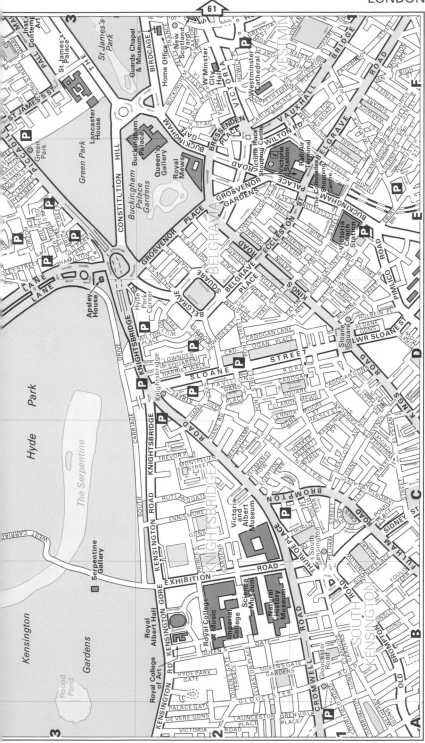

LONDON

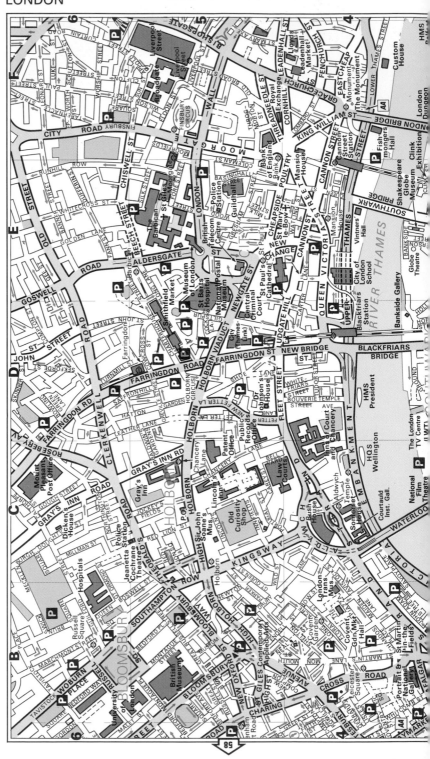

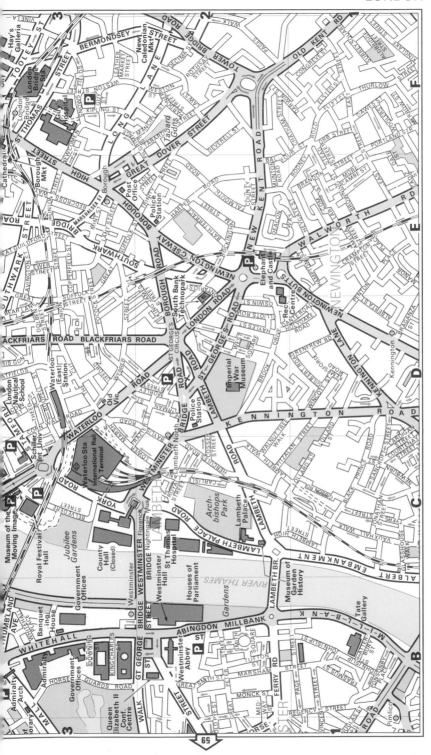

MANCHESTER

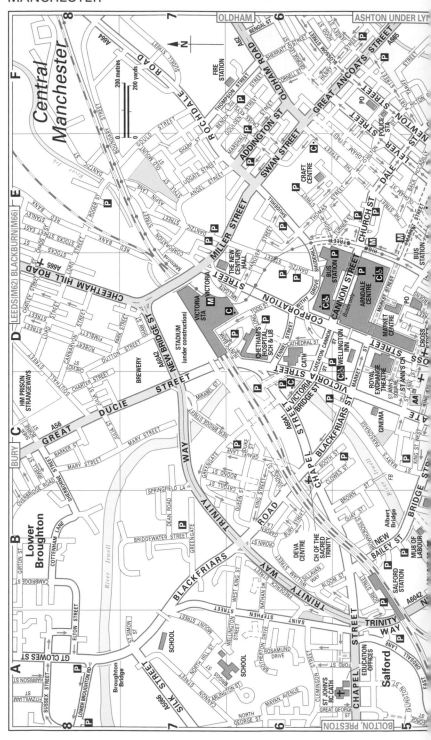

MANCHESTER

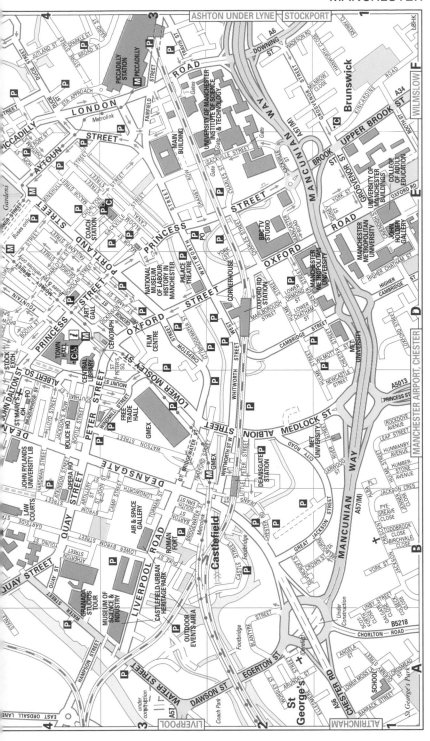

MAIDENHEAD MAIDSTONE

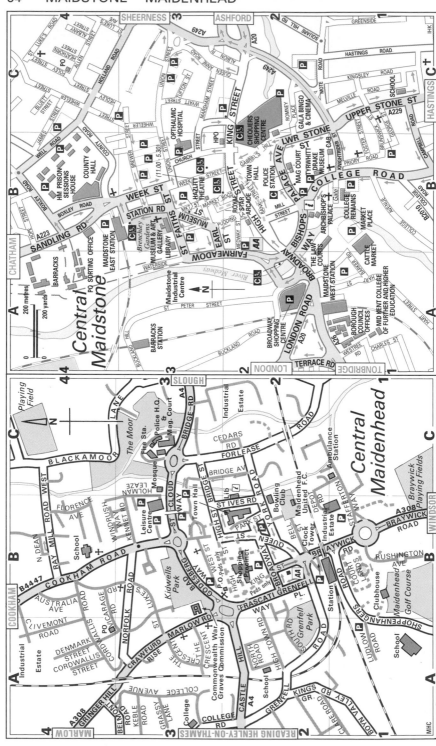

MIDDLESBROUGH

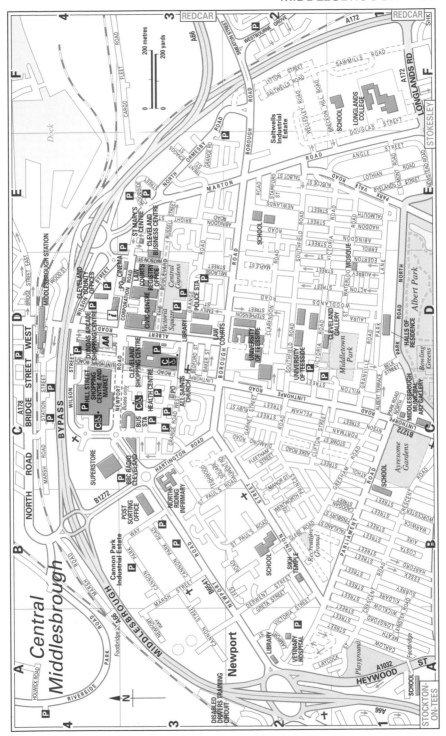

MILTON KEYNES

Central Milton Keynes

200 metres
200 yards

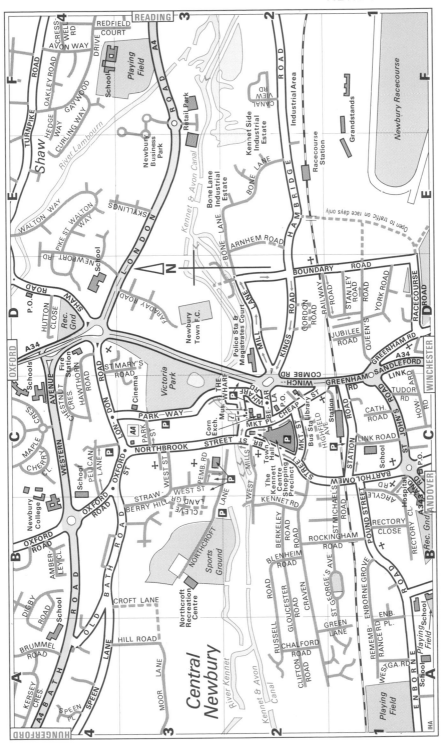

NEWBURY

NEWCASTLE UPON TYNE

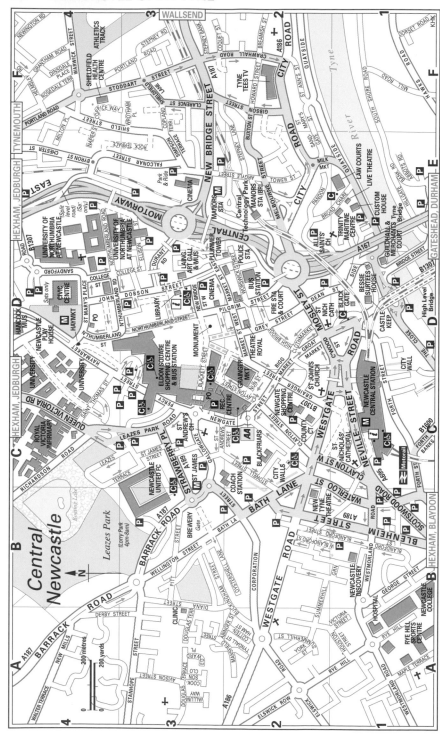

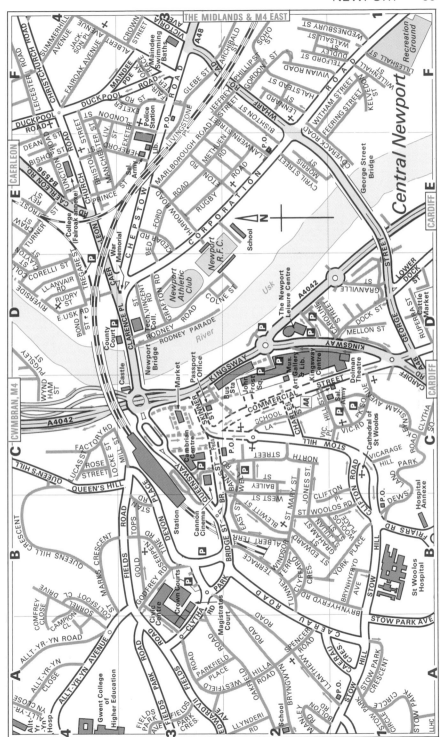

NEWPORT

Central Newport

NEWPORT NEWCASTLE UNDER LYME

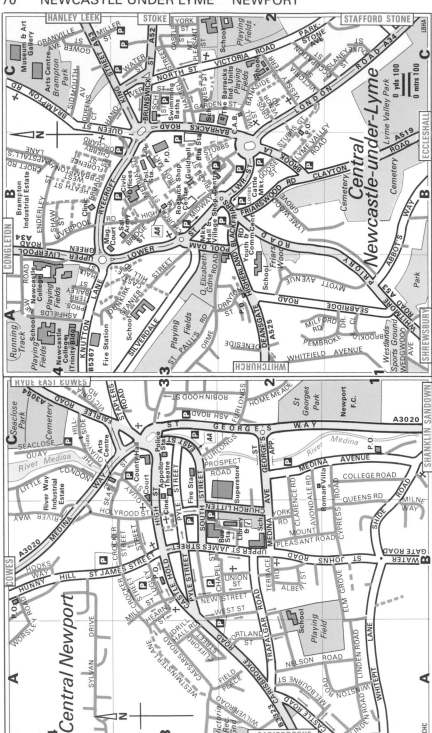

Central Newcastle-under-Lyme

Central Newport

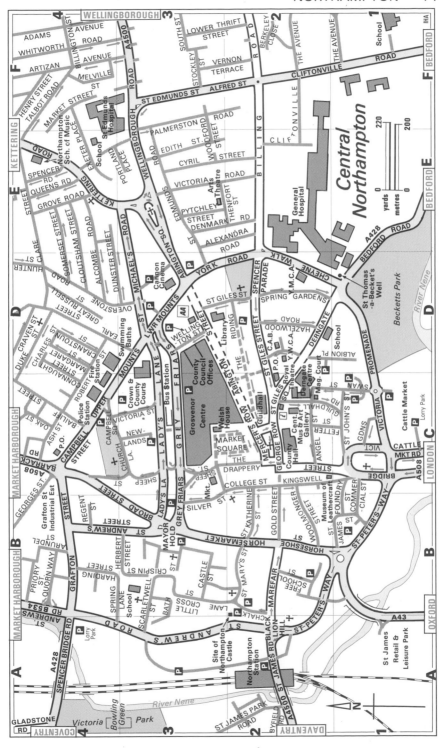

NORTHAMPTON

Central Northampton

NORWICH

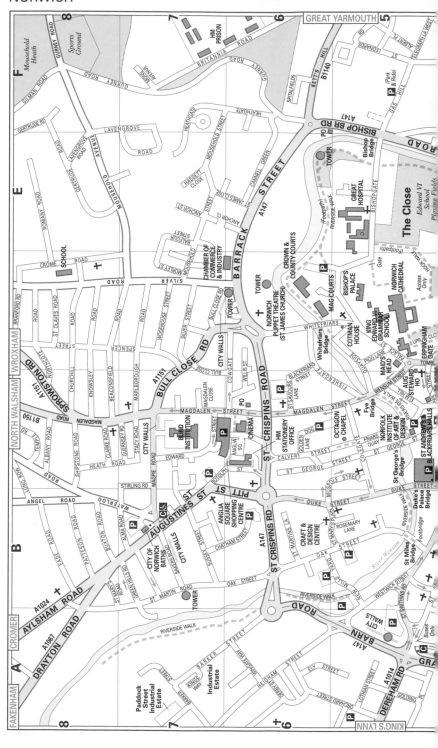

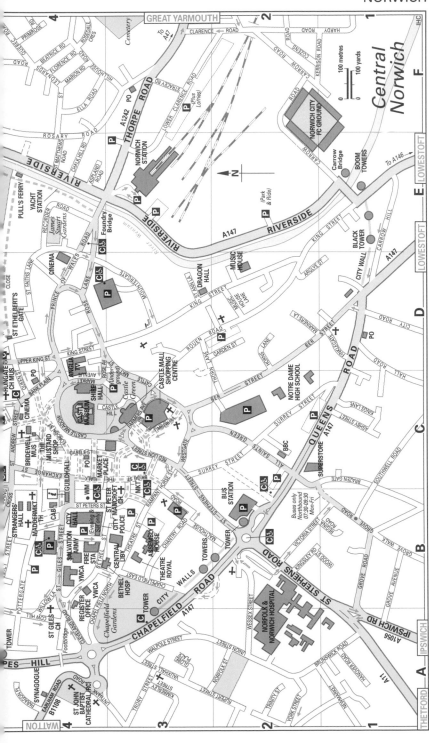

NORWICH

Central Norwich

NOTTINGHAM

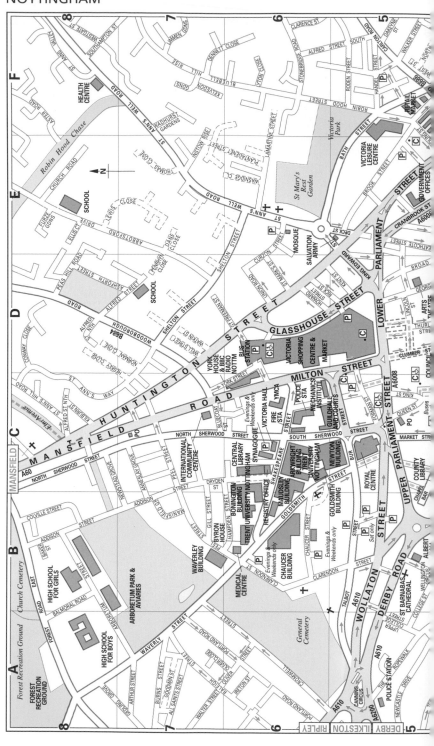

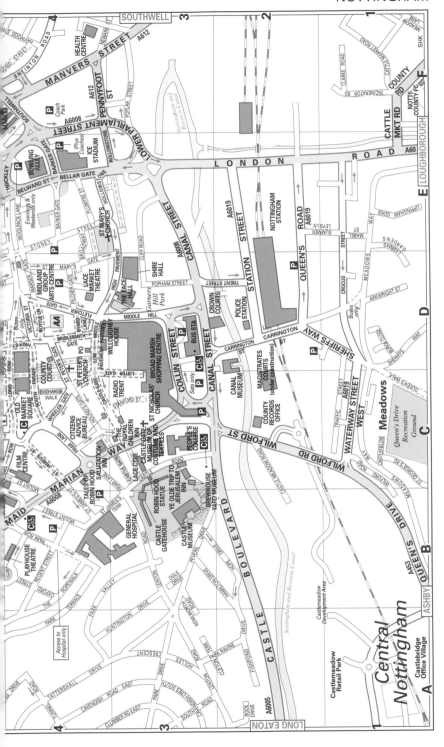

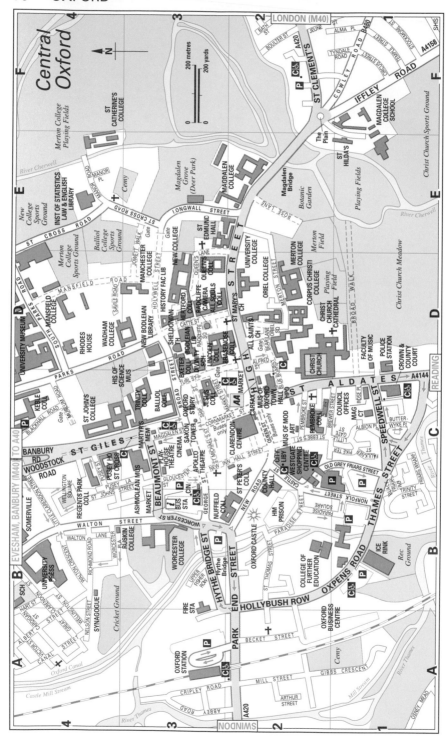

OXFORD

Central Oxford

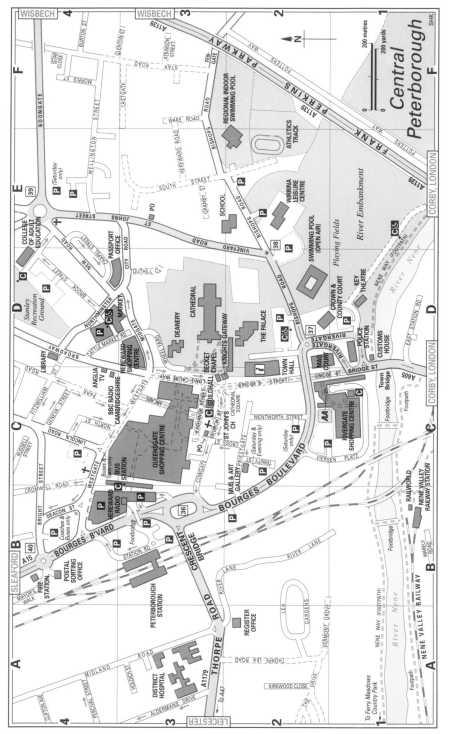

PETERBOROUGH

Central Peterborough

200 metres
200 yards

WISBECH 4
WISBECH 3
A1139
FRANK PERKINS PARKWAY
POTTERS WAY
FEN GATE

REGIONAL INDOOR SWIMMING POOL
ATHLETICS TRACK
WAKE ROAD
SCHOOL
SOUTH STREET
STAR CLOSE
STAR ROAD
BURTON ST
MORRIS ST
GLENTON ST
ATKINSON STREET
EASTGATE
HEREWARD ROAD
BISHOPS ROAD
GRANBY ST
VINEYARD ROAD
BOONGATE
WELLINGTON STREET

WIRRINA LEISURE CENTRE
SWIMMING POOL (OPEN AIR)
River Embankment
River Nene
Playing Fields
KEY THEATRE

ST JOHNS STREET
COLLEGE OF ADULT EDUCATION
PASSPORT OFFICE
CITY ROAD
TOUTHILL CL
CATHEDRAL
DEANERY
WHEEL YARD
KNIGHTS GATEWAY
BECKET CHAPEL
THE PALACE
CROWN & COUNTY COURT
POLICE STATION
CUSTOMS HOUSE
RIVERGATE
BRIDGE ST
BISHOPS ROAD
EAST STATION RD

Stanley Recreation Ground
NORTHMINSTER
MARKET
CHAPEL STREET
NEW ROAD
BROOK STREET
CATTLE MARKET RD
HEREWARD SHOPPING CENTRE
MIDGATE
LONG CAUSEWAY
ARCADE
EXCHANGE STREET
CATHEDRAL SQUARE
TOWN HALL
MAG COURT
BRIDGE ST
BRIDGE STREET
Town Bridge
Footbridge
Footpath

LIBRARY
BROADWAY
FITZWILLIAM ROAD
GENEVA STREET
NORTH ST
LINCOLN ROAD
ANGLIA TV
BBC RADIO CAMBRIDGESHIRE
WESTGATE
ST JOHN'S
CHURCH ST
CROSS ST
WENTWORTH STREET
PRIESTGATE
COWGATE
BRIDGE'S STREET
QUEENSGATE SHOPPING CENTRE
MUS & ART GALLERY
BOURGES BOULEVARD
RIVERGATE SHOPPING CENTRE
VIERSEN PLATZ
AA
RAILWORLD
NENE VALLEY RAILWAY STATION

RUSSELL STREET
CROMWELL ROAD
BRIGHT ST
DEACON ST
HEREWARD RADIO
WESTGATE
BUS STATION
Coaches & Buses only
Footbridge
STATION RD
BOURGES B'VARD
A15
SLEAFORD
MAYOR'S WALK
FIRE STATION
POSTAL SORTING OFFICE
PETERBOROUGH STATION
CRESCENT BRIDGE
THORPE ROAD
RIVER LANE
RIVER LANE
LEA
GARDENS
VERMONT GROVE
REGISTER OFFICE
River Nene
NENE WAY (FOOTPATH)

DISTRICT HOSPITAL
HOLROYD ST
PERCIVAL STREET
CLIFTON AVE
MIDLAND ROAD
A1179
ALDERMANS DRIVE
KIRKWOOD CLOSE
THORPE LEA ROAD
THE DRIVE
To Ferry Meadows Country Park
NENE VALLEY RAILWAY
LEICESTER 3
To A47

CORBY, LONDON
A1139
A605
CORBY, LONDON
WARLEY ROAD

PLYMOUTH

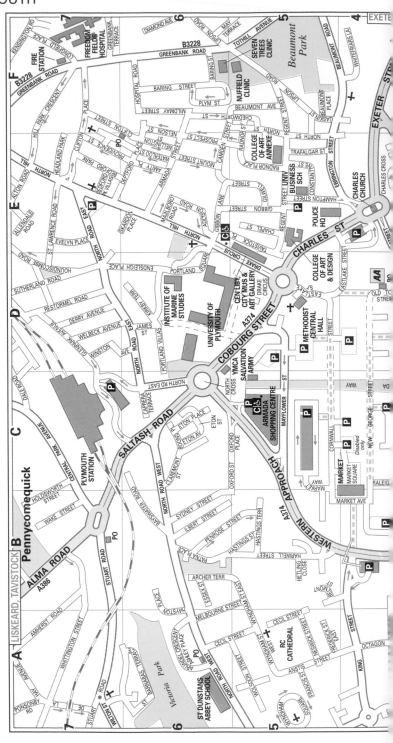

PLYMOUTH

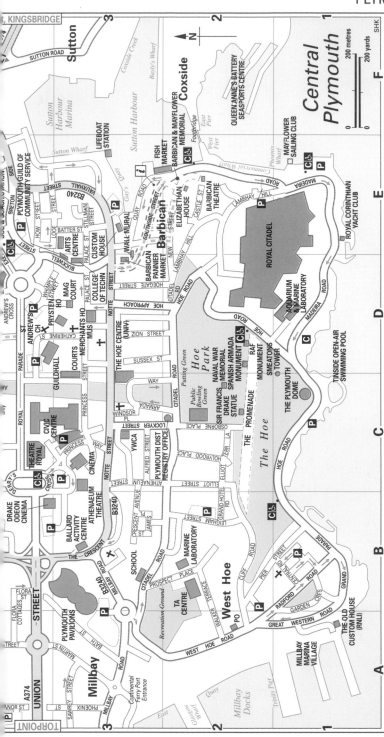

Central Plymouth

N

200 metres
200 yards

SHK

Sutton

Coxside

Barbican

The Hoe

Hoe Park

West Hoe

Millbay

Millbay Docks

Sutton Harbour

Sutton Harbour Marina

KINGSBRIDGE

TORPOINT

A374

UNION STREET

PLYMOUTH PAVILIONS

DRAKE ODEON CINEMA

THEATRE ROYAL

CIVIC CENTRE

GUILDHALL

ATHENAEUM THEATRE

BALLARD ACTIVITY CENTRE

YWCA

MARINE LABORATORY

TA CENTRE

THE HOE CENTRE

CIVIC CENTRE

PLYMOUTH DIST REGISTRY OFFICE

WINDSOR PL

SIR FRANCIS DRAKE STATUE

NAVAL WAR MEMORIAL

SPANISH ARMADA MONUMENT

RAF MONUMENT

SMEATONS TOWER

THE PLYMOUTH DOME

THE PROMENADE

TINSIDE OPEN-AIR SWIMMING POOL

AQUARIUM & MARINE LABORATORY

ROYAL CITADEL

ROYAL CORINTHIAN YACHT CLUB

MAYFLOWER SAILING CLUB

QUEEN ANNE'S BATTERY SEASPORTS CENTRE

BARBICAN THEATRE

ELIZABETHAN HOUSE

BARBICAN PANNIER MARKET

ARTS CENTRE

CUSTOM HOUSE

MAG COURT

MERCHANTS HO MUS

COLLEGE OF TECHN

WALL MURAL

FISH MARKET

BARBICAN & MAYFLOWER MEMORIAL

LIFEBOAT STATION

PLYMOUTH GUILD OF COMMUNITY SERVICE

PRYSTEN HO

COURTS

THE OLD CUSTOM HOUSE (RNLI)

MILLBAY MARINA VILLAGE

SCHOOL

PO

Continental Ferry Port Entrance

PERTH POOLE

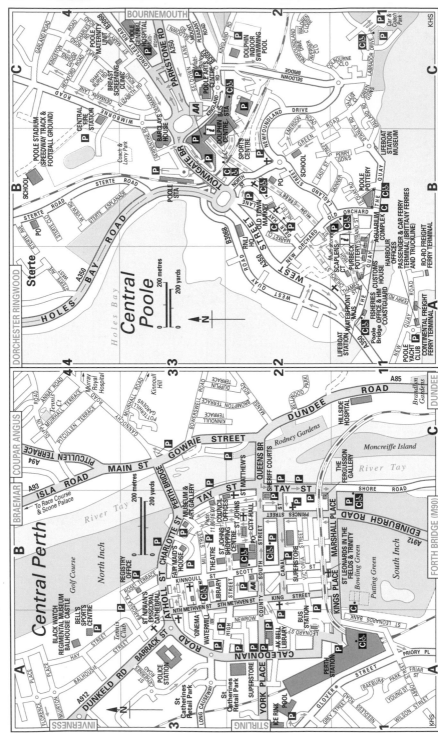

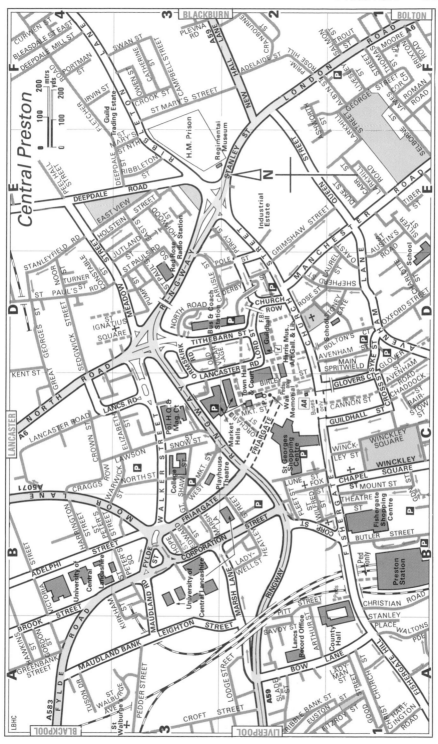

PRESTON

Central Preston

PORTSMOUTH

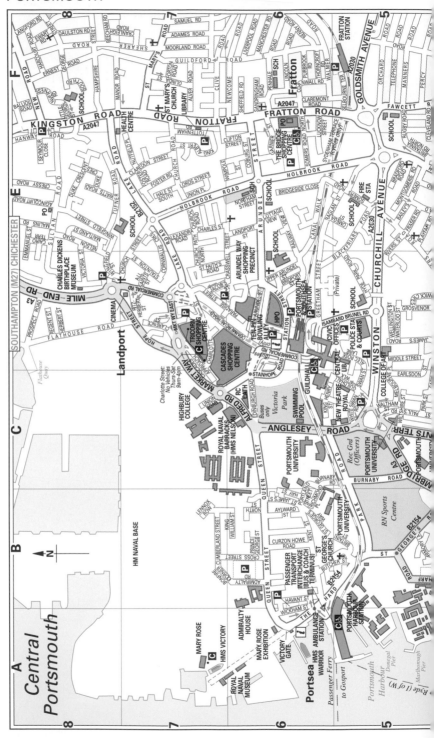

Central Portsmouth

PORTSMOUTH

REDDITCH RAMSGATE

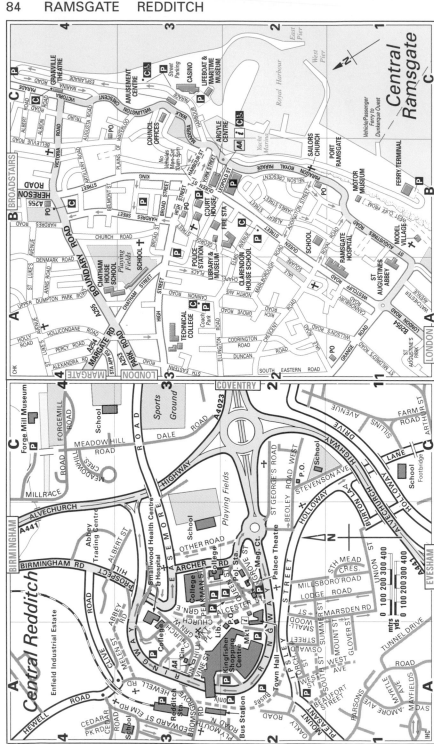

Central Ramsgate

Central Redditch

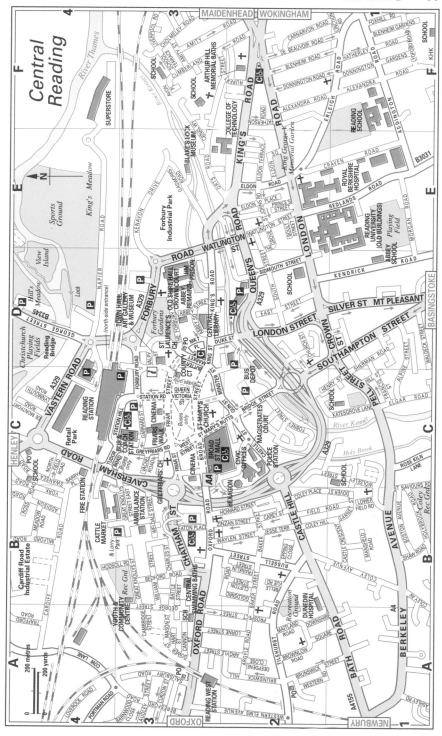

REIGATE

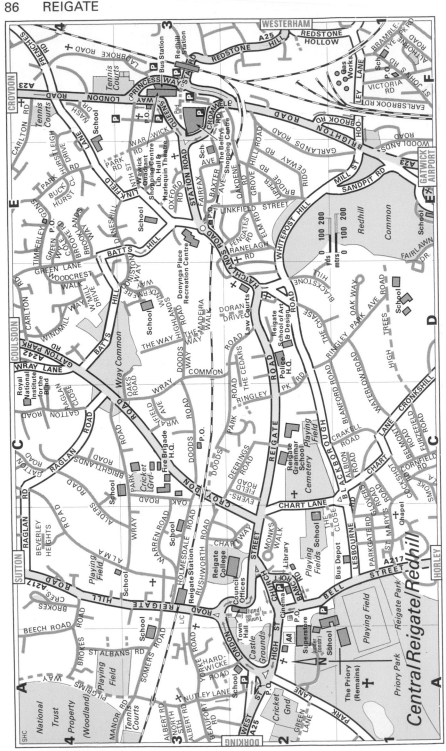

RUGBY RIPON

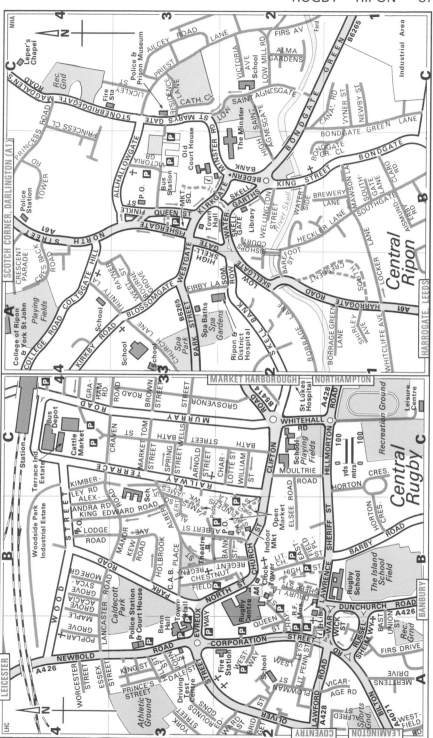

ROCHDALE

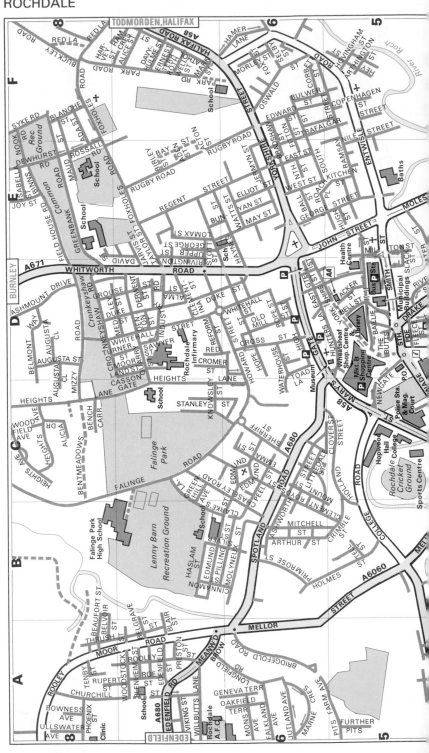

ST ANDREWS

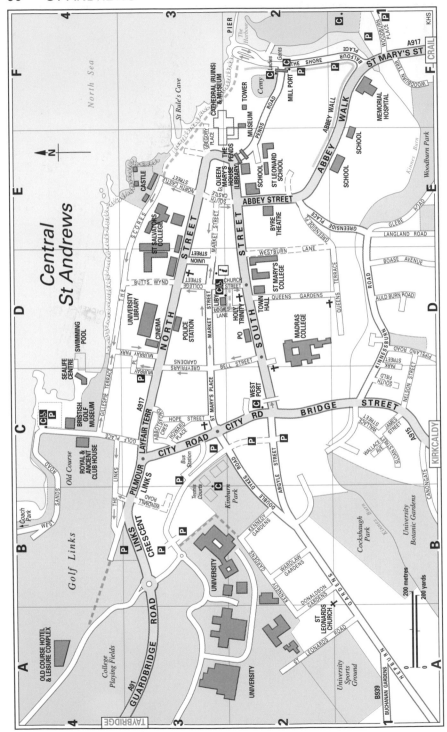

Central St Andrews

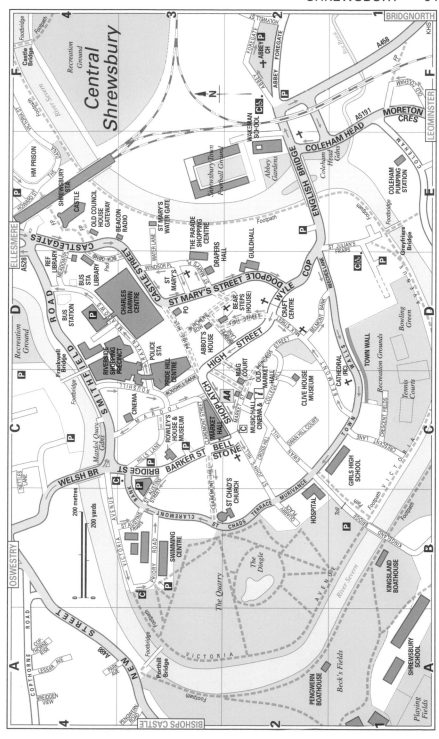

SHREWSBURY

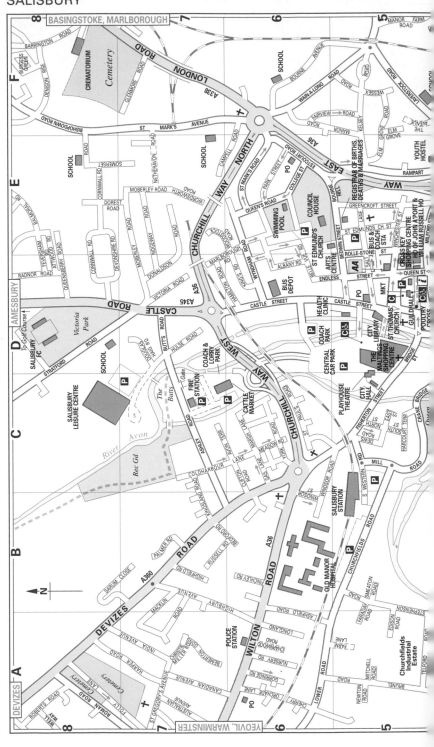

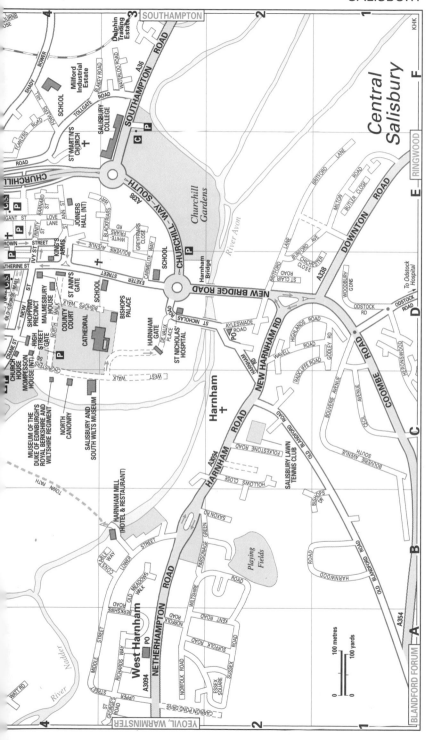

SALISBURY

Central Salisbury

SHEFFIELD

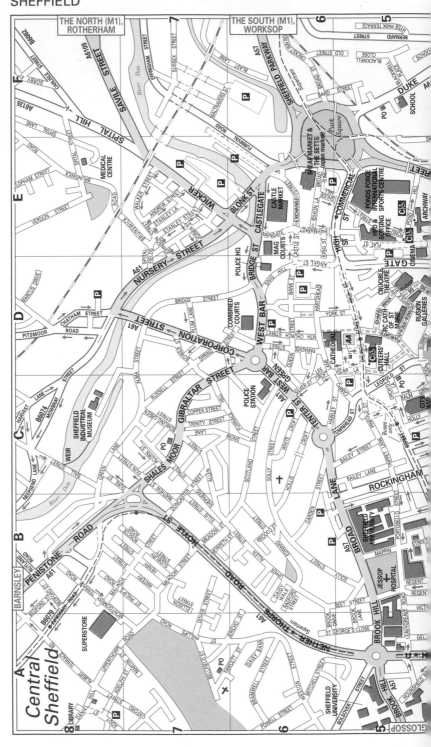

Central Sheffield

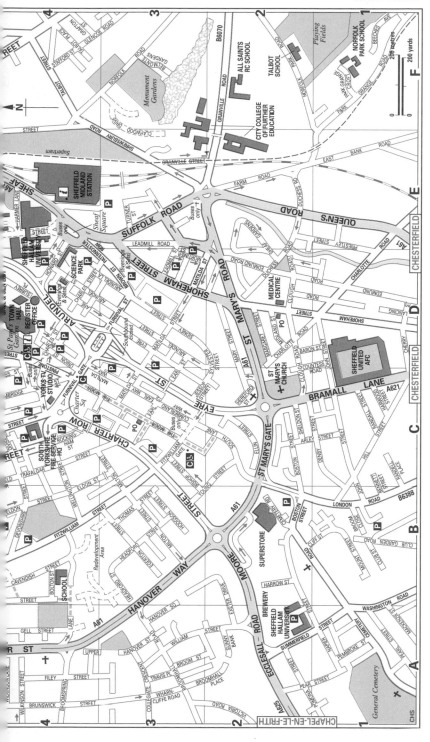

SHEFFIELD

SLOUGH

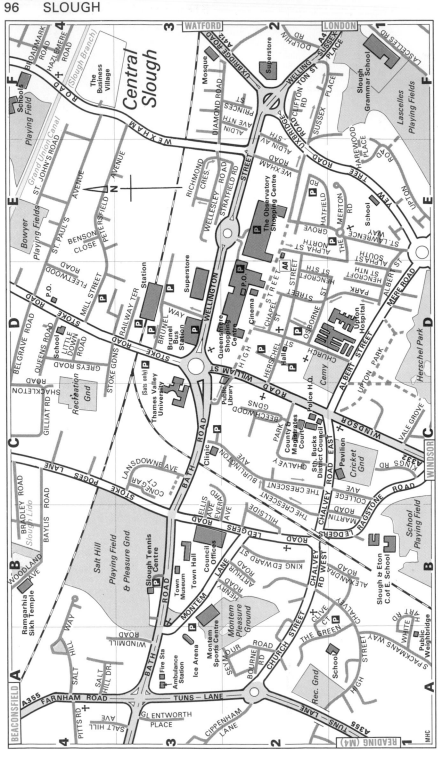

Central Slough

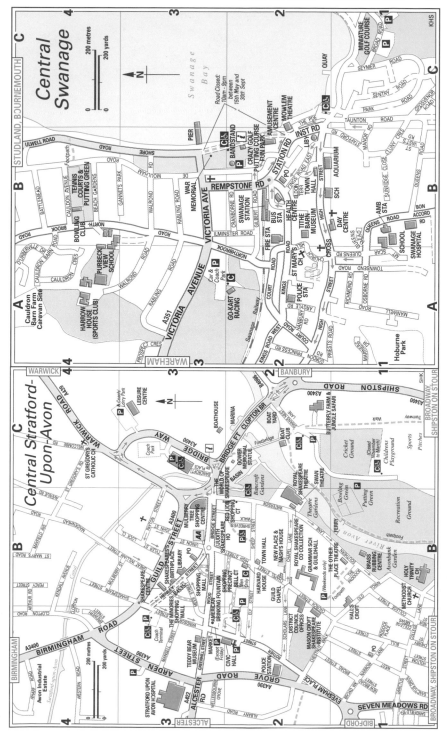

STRATFORD SWANAGE

SOUTHAMPTON

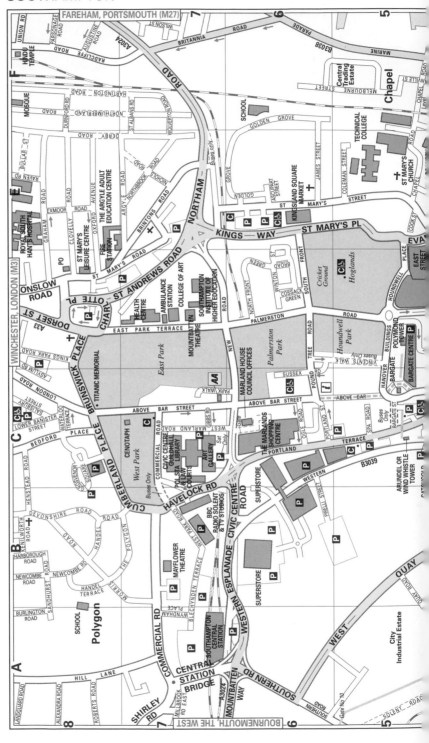

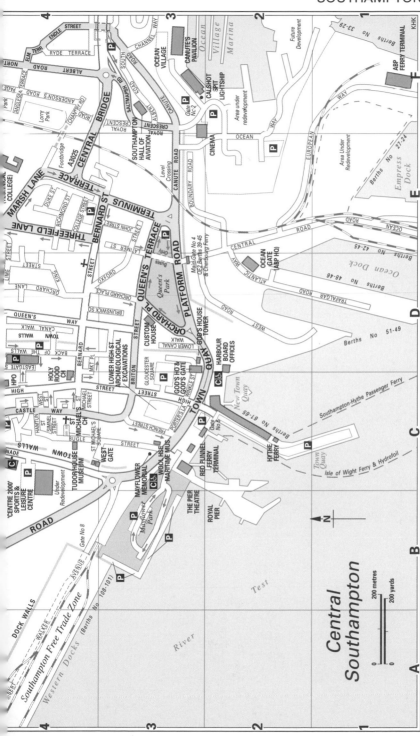

SOUTHAMPTON

Central
Southampton

SUNDERLAND

Central Sunderland

Port of Sunderland

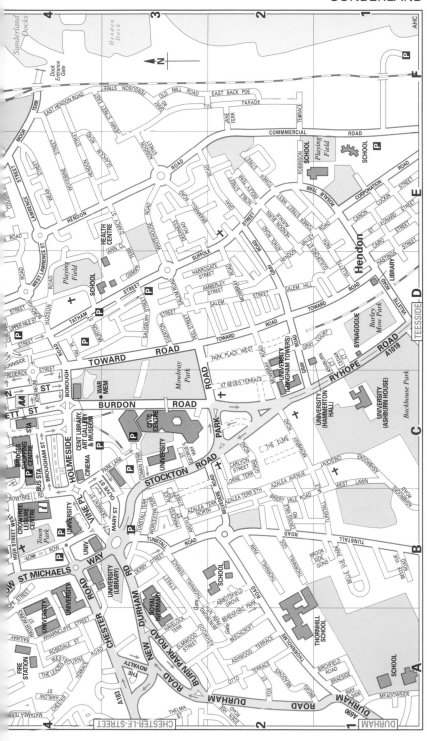

SUNDERLAND

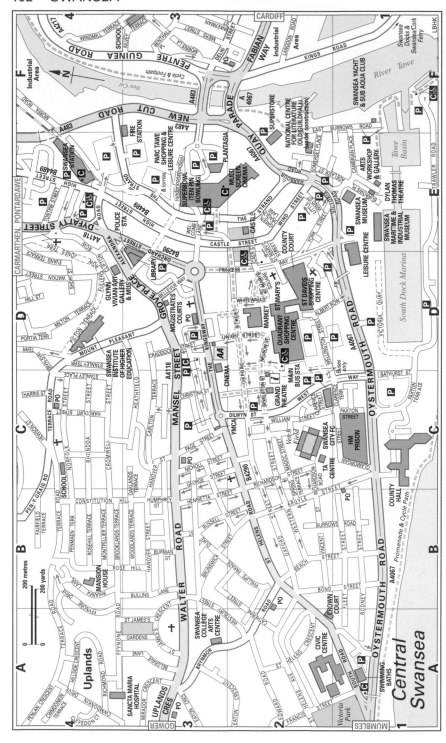

SWANSEA

SWINDON

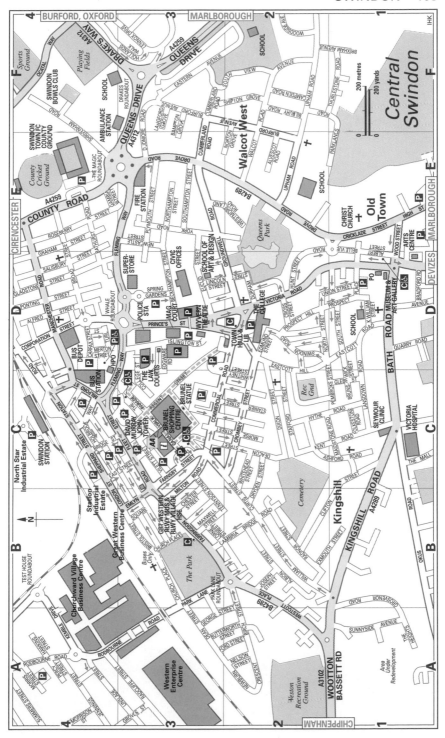

Central Swindon

WARWICK WINDSOR

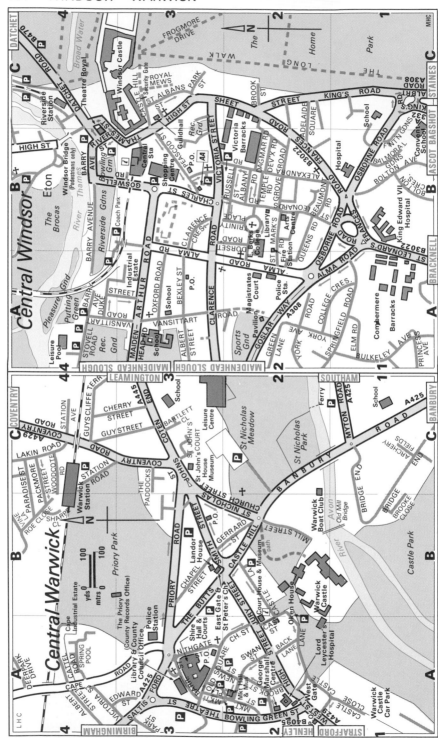

WINDSOR

Central Windsor

DATCHET
STAINES A308
ASCOT BAGSHOT
BRACKNELL
MAIDENHEAD SLOUGH

FROGMORE DRIVE
Broad Water
Windsor Castle
Theatre Royal
Riverside Station
Eton
The Brocas
River Thames
Windsor Bridge (Pedestrians only)
ROYAL MEWS
Security Gate
CASTLE HILL
ST ALBANS PARK
HIGH ST
Guildhall
Rec Grd
Central Sta
Shopping Centre
Bowling Grn
Pleasure Grnd
Riverside Gdns
Coach Park
Putting Green
Leisure Pool
SHEET ST
BROOK ST
KING'S ROAD
STREET
Victoria Barracks
Hospital
ADELAIDE SQUARE
OSBORNE ROAD
BALMORAL GDNS
CONVENT AVE
BOLTON CRES
King Edward VII Hospital
A332
FNTN GDNS
Library
Arts Centre
Fire Station
St Mark's
St Leonard's
Queens Rd
Alma Road
Magistrates Court
Police Sta.
P.O.
Sports Grnd
Pavilion
GOSLAR WAY A308
COLLEGE CRES.
SPRINGFIELD ROAD
YORK AVE
ELM RD
Barracks
Combermere
BULKELEY AVE
PRINCESS AVE
Industrial Estate
Oxford Road
Bexley St
Vansittart
ALBERT STREET
MAIDENHEAD RD
STOVELL ROAD
Rec. Grnd
DUKE ST
BARRY AVE
The
N

WARWICK

Central Warwick

COVENTRY
LEAMINGTON
SOUTHAM
BANBURY
BIRMINGHAM
HENLEY
STRATFORD

STATION AVE
CHERRY STREET
GUY STREET
A445
COTEN END
School
St John's Court House Museum
St Nicholas Meadow
St Nicholas Park
Ferry
MYTON ROAD A425
School
ARCHERY FIELDS
Warwick Station
COVENTRY ROAD A429
LAKIN ROAD
VINE ST
PARADISE ST
PACKMORE ST
WOODCOTE RD
ROE CLOSE
SHARPE CL
The Priory (County Records Office)
Priory Park
Police Station
Cape Industrial Estate
Library & County Council Office
THE PADDOCKS
PRIORY ROAD
ST JOHN'S
SMITH STREET
THE BUTTS
CHAPEL STREET
Landor House
St Nicholas Church St
Leisure Centre
BARTLETT CL
St Peter's Ch
East Gate & Court House & Museum
Shire Hall & Courts
Oken House
GERRARD ST
CASTLE HILL
CASTLE LANE
MILL STREET
Warwick Boat Club
Old Mill Bridge
River Avon
Warwick Castle
Lord Leicester's Hospital
Castle Park
BRIDGE END
BROOKE CLOSE
Warwick Castle Car Park
NITHGATE
SWAN ST
MARKET PLACE
George Marshall Centre
Mkt Hall & Mus
BROOK ST
HIGH ST
West Gate
BOWLING GREEN ST
THEATRE ST
BACK LANE
WEST ST A4189
CASTLE ST
CASTLE CLOSE
SALTISFORD
CAPE ROAD
DEEPARK DRIVE
SPRING POOL
ALBERT STREET
VICTORIA ST
PARK ST
EDWARD ST
A425
yds 0 100
mtrs 0 100
N

MHC
LHC

WEMBLEY

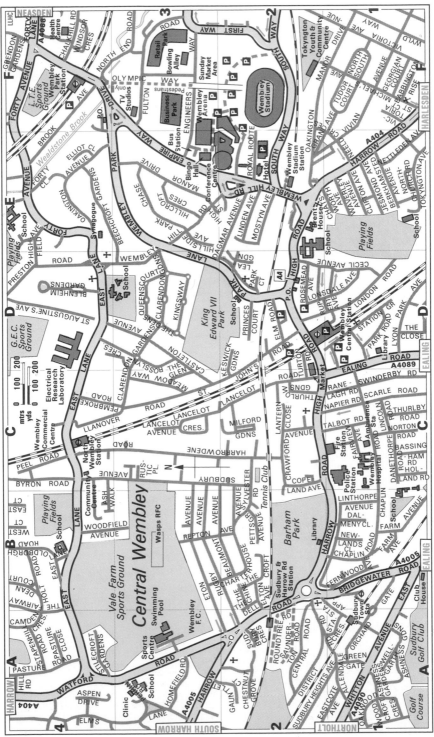

WEST BROMWICH

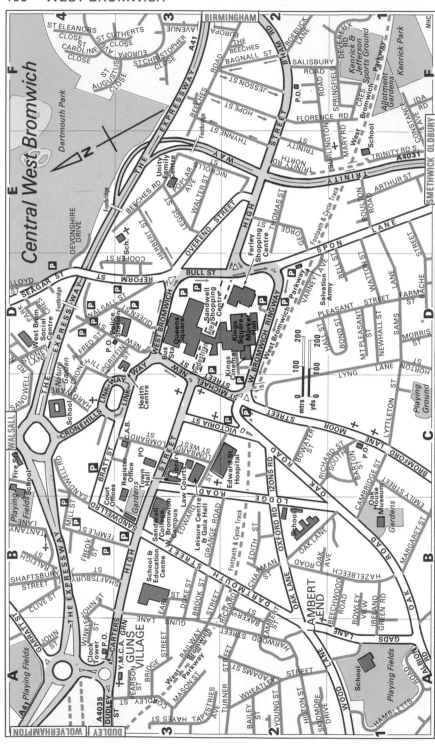

Central West Bromwich

WEYMOUTH

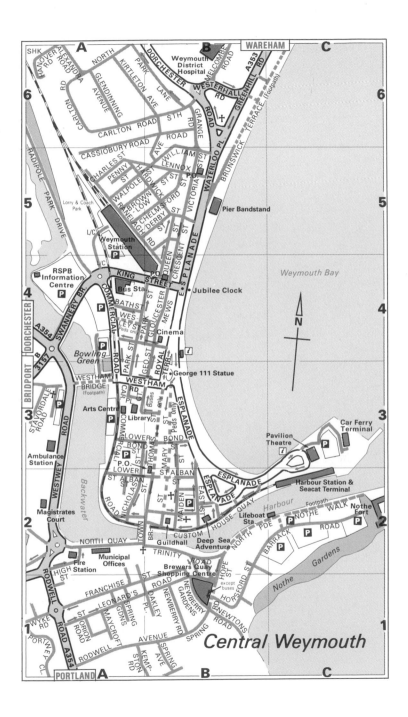

Central Weymouth

WINCHESTER

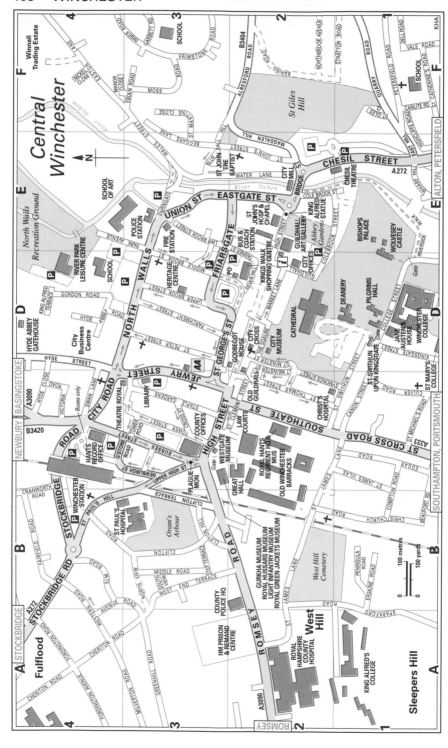

Central Winchester

Winnall Trading Estate

School

Frimstone

Moss

St Giles Hill

School

St John's Ball

Magdalen Hill

St John The Baptist

Water Lane

City Mill

Chesil Theatre

CHESIL STREET A272

ALTON, PETERSFIELD

North Walls Recreation Ground

School of Art

Police Station

River Park Leisure Centre

Fire Station

Heritage Centre

UNION ST

EASTGATE ST

FRIARSGATE

Bus & Coach Station

St John's Hosp & Chapel

Guildhall City Art Gallery

Abbey Gardens

King Alfred Statue

Bishops Palace

Wolvesey Castle

Kings Walk Shopping Centre

City Offices

DEANERY

Pilgrims Hall

Hyde Abbey Gatehouse

City Business Centre

Gordon Road

King Alfred Terrace

NORTH WALLS

Parchment Street

St Peter Street

St George's St

Godbegot House

City Cross

City Museum

CATHEDRAL

Jane Austen's House

Winchester College

St Mary's College

NEWBURY / BASINGSTOKE B3420

CITY ROAD

Theatre Royal

JEWRY STREET

Library

County Offices

Old Guildhall

Christ's Hospital

St Swithun Upon Kingsgate

HIGH STREET

SOUTHGATE ST

ST CROSS ROAD A333

SOUTHAMPTON, PORTSMOUTH

STOCKBRIDGE ROAD

Hants Record Office

Winchester Station

HIGH STREET

Plague Mon

Westgate Museum

Great Hall

Royal Hants Regiment HQ & Mus

Old Winchester Barracks

Law Courts

STOCKBRIDGE A272

Fulflood

Cranworth Road

St Paul's Hospital

Oram's Arbour

Gurkha Museum
Royal Hussars Museum
Light Infantry Museum
Royal Green Jackets Museum

West Hill Cemetery

County Police Ho

HM Prison & Remand Centre

ROMSEY ROAD A3090

Royal Hampshire County Hospital

West Hill

King Alfred's College

Sleepers Hill

ROMSEY

100 metres
100 yards

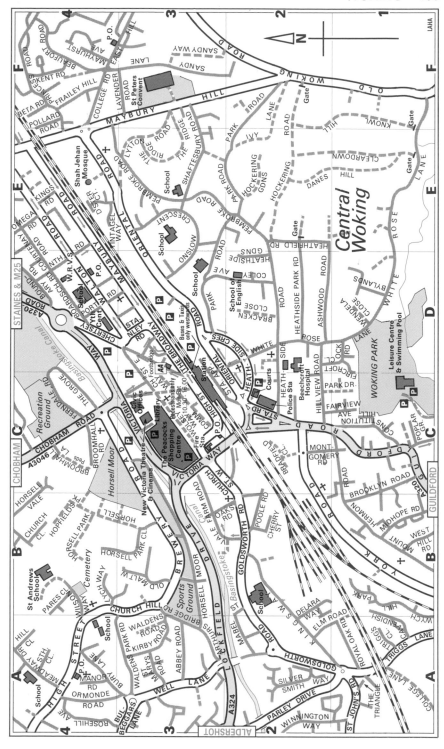

WOKING

WOLVERHAMPTON

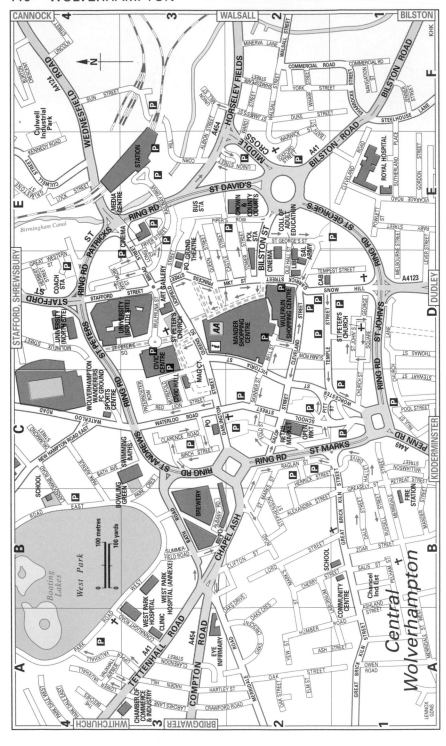

WORCESTER

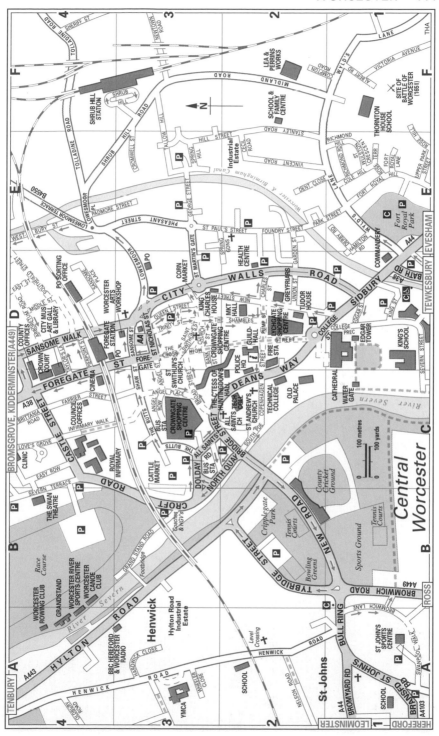

Central Worcester

YORK

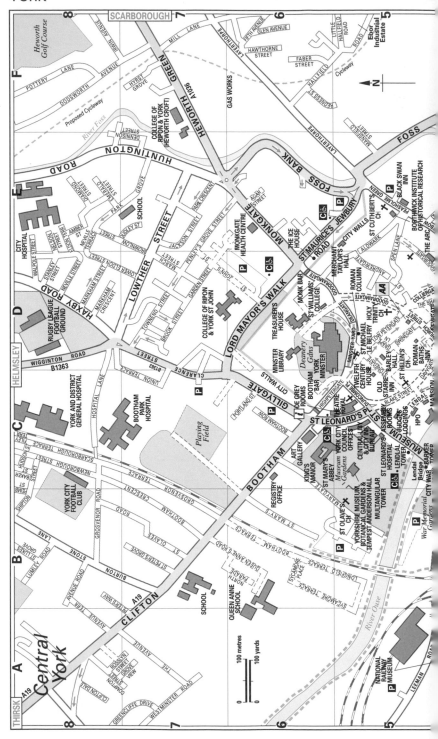

YORK

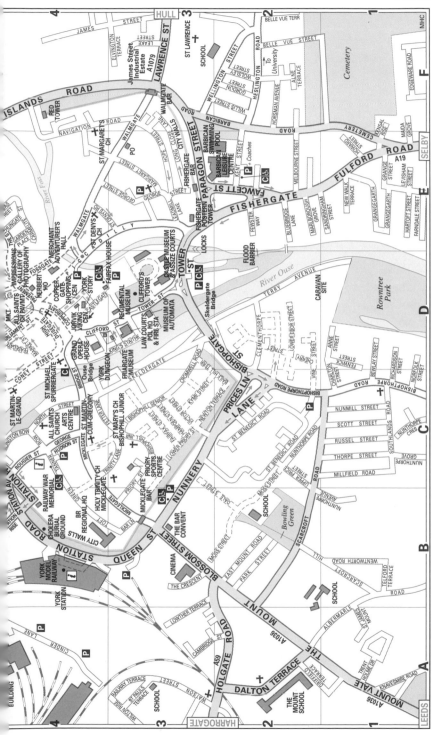

BELFAST

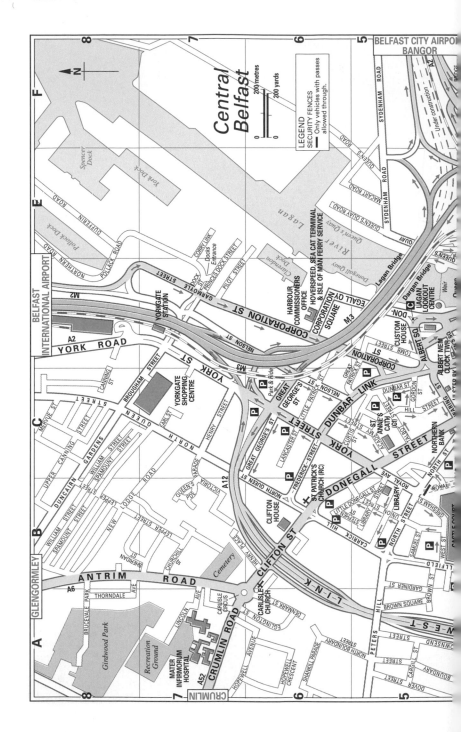

Central Belfast

LEGEND
SECURITY FENCES
— Only vehicles with passes allowed through.

BELFAST CITY AIRPORT
BANGOR

BELFAST INTERNATIONAL AIRPORT

YORK ROAD

ANTRIM ROAD

CRUMLIN ROAD

MATER INFIRMORUM HOSPITAL

Girdwood Park

Recreation Ground

CLIFTON HOUSE

CARLISLE CIRCUS

CARLISLE CHURCH

YORKGATE SHOPPING CENTRE

YORKGATE STATION

HARBOUR COMMISSIONERS OFFICE

HOVERSPEED, SEA CAT TERMINAL & ISLE OF MAN FERRY SERVICE

CORPORATION SQUARE

CORPORATION ST

CUSTOM HOUSE

ALBERT SQ

ALBERT MEM CLOCK TWR

LAGAN LOOKOUT CENTRE

DUNBAR LINK

ST ANNE'S CATH (CI)

ST PATRICK'S CHURCH (RC)

DONEGALL STREET

Lagan Bridge

River Lagan

Queen's Quay

Spencer Dock

York Dock

Pollock Dock

Dargan Bridge

BELFAST

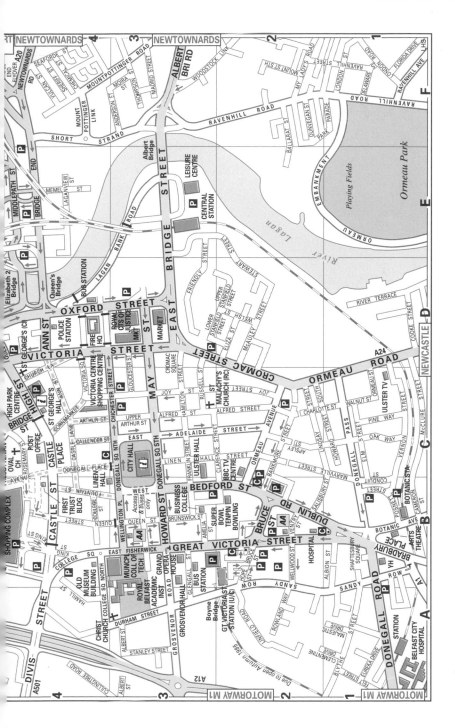

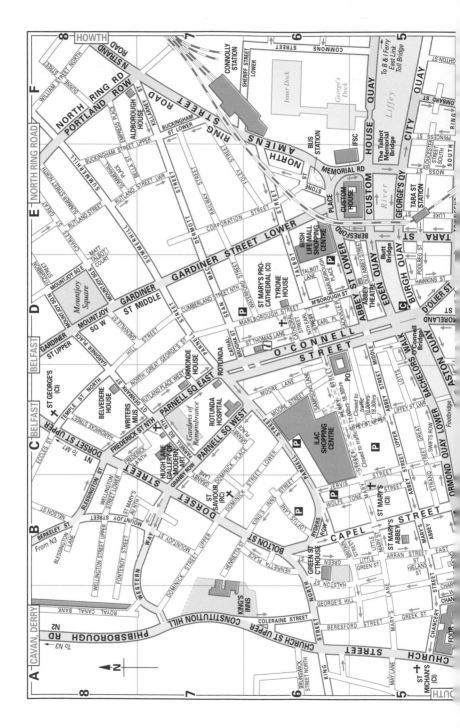

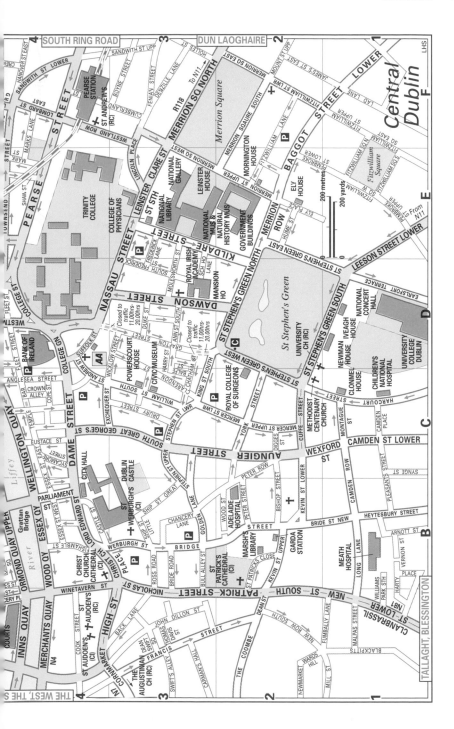

DUBLIN

Central Dublin

LHS

F

E

D

C

B

SOUTH RING ROAD

DUN LAOGHAIRE

THE WEST, THE S

TALLAGHT, BLESSINGTON

HEATHROW AIRPORT   GATWICK AIRPORT

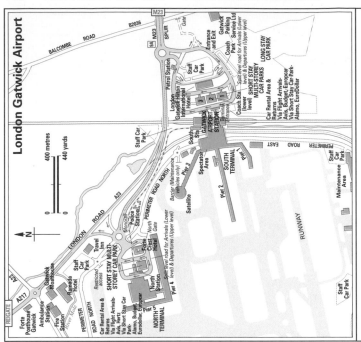

London Gatwick Airport

Gatwick Airport - 28 miles south of London

Telephone: 01293 535353

Parking: Short and Long-stay parking available at both the North and South terminal. For charge details tel: 01293 502390 (short-stay) and either 0800 128128 or 01293 569222 (long stay)

Public Transport: Coach, Bus and Rail. There are several 4-star and 3-star hotels within easy reach of the airport and car hire facilities are available

Heathrow Airport

Heathrow Airport - 16 miles west of London

Telephone: 0181 759 4321

Parking: Short-stay, Long-stay and business parking available. For charge details tel: 0181 745 7160

Public Transport: Coach, Bus and London Underground
There are several 4-star and 3-star hotels within easy reach of the airport and car hire facilities are available

STANSTED AIRPORT   LUTON AIRPORT

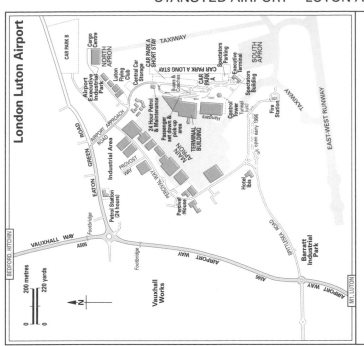

London Luton Airport

CAR PARK B

Cargo Centre

NORTH APRON

TAXIWAY

Airport Executive Industrial Park

Luton Flying Club

Central Car Storage

CAR PARK A SHORT STAY

Spectators Parking

Executive Terminal

SOUTH APRON

CAR PARK A LONG STAY

Buses & Coaches

Spectators Building

Industrial Area

24-Hour Petrol & Maintenance

Passenger set down & pick-up area

Hangars

MAIN APRON

TERMINAL BUILDING

Control Tower

Tunnel (u/c)

Fire Station

due open early 1996

TAXIWAY

EAST-WEST RUNWAY

Petrol Station (24 hours)

Footbridge

Hotel Ibis

Percival House

PROVOST WAY

PERCIVAL WAY

AIRPORT APPROACH ROAD

EATON GREEN ROAD

VAUXHALL WAY

A505

Footbridge

SPITTLESEA ROAD

AIRPORT WAY

A505

AIRPORT WAY

Barratt Industrial Park

Vauxhall Works

BEDFORD, HITCHIN

M1, LUTON

0   200 metres
0   220 yards

N

London Luton Airport - 35 miles north of London

Telephone: 01582 405100
Parking: Short and Long-stay open air parking available
Public Transport: Coach, Bus and Rail
There is one 2-star hotel at the airport and several 3-star hotels within easy reach of the airport. Car hire facilities are available

London Stansted Airport

CAMBRIDGE

M11

Tye Green

CLAVDI HILL

BELFER ROAD

TYE GREEN ROAD

Burton End

Maintenance Area

Fire Service Training Area

BUSINESS AVIATION CENTRE

Car Park

RUNWAY

MOLEHILL GREEN ROUNDABOUT

TERMINAL ROAD SOUTH

TERMINAL ROAD NORTH

SHORT STAY CAR PARK

Car Rental Returns

COACH PARK

SHORT STAY CAR PARK

PASSENGER TERMINAL & RAILWAY STATION

Satellite

Transit Link

Gate

Satellite

Police Sta

Enterprise House

Cargo Area

Gate

Fire Sta

COOPERS END ROUNDABOUT

Cooper's End

BASSINGBOURN RD

LONG BORDER RD

THREMHALL AVE

BASSINGBOURN ROUNDABOUT

Taylors End

No access to terminal

Maintenance Area

Maintenance Area

RUNWAY

Priory Wood

THREMHALL AVENUE

DUNMOW ROAD

COLCHESTER

A120

Puse's Brook

DUNMOW ROAD

Takeley Street

Hatfield Forest (Country Park)

LONG STAY CAR PARK

BURY LODGE LANE

Hilton National Hotel

PRIORY WOOD ROUNDABOUT

ROUND COPPICE ROAD

A120

Petrol Station

Start Hill

Footbridge

A1250

BIRCHANGER LANE

CHURCH RD

M11

M11

LONDON

Stansted Park

Stansted Hall

BISHOPS STORTFORD

0   400 metres
0   440 yards

N

London Stansted Airport - 38 miles north-east of London

Telephone: 01279 680500
Parking: Short and Long-stay open air parking available. For charge details tel: 01279 662373
Public Transport: Coach, Bus and a direct Rail link to London on the 'Stansted Express'
There are several 4-star and 3-star hotels within easy reach of the airport and car hire facilities are available

LONDON CITY AIRPORT   BIRMINGHAM AIRPORT

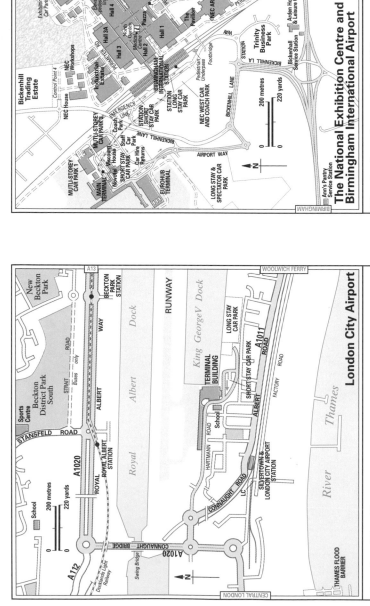

The National Exhibition Centre and Birmingham International Airport

Birmingham International Airport - 8 miles east of of Birmingham

Telephone: 0121 767 5511 (Main Terminal), 0121 767 7502 (Eurohub Terminal)
Parking: Short and Long-stay parking available
For charge details tel: 0121 767 7861
Public Transport: Bus Service. Maglev transit system offers a 90 second shuttle service to Birmingham International Railway Station
There are several 3-star hotels within easy reach of the airport and car hire facilities are available

London City Airport

London City Airport - 6 miles east of London

Telephone: 0171 474 5555
Parking: Short and Long-stay parking available
Public Transport: 'Shuttlebus' service into London. Easy access to Rail network and London Underground
There is a 4-star and 2-star hotel within easy reach of the airport and car hire facilities are available

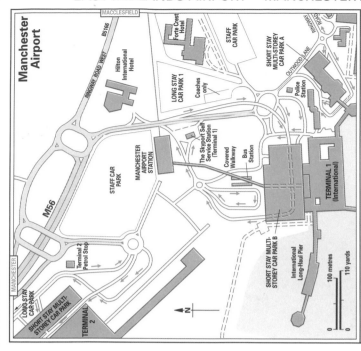

Manchester Airport - 10 miles south of Manchester

Telephone: 0161 489 3000
Parking: Short and Long-stay parking available.
Public Transport: Bus, Coach and Rail. Manchester airport railway station connects with the Rail network
There are several 4-star and 3-star hotels within easy reach of the airport and car hire facilities are available

East Midlands International Airport
15 miles southwest of Nottingham. Next to the M1 at junctions 23A and 24

Telephone: 01332 852852
Parking: Short and Long-stay parking available
Public Transport: Bus and coach services to major towns and cities in the East Midlands
There are several 3-star hotels in easy reach of the airport and car hire facilities are available

EDINBURGH AIRPORT GLASGOW AIRPORT

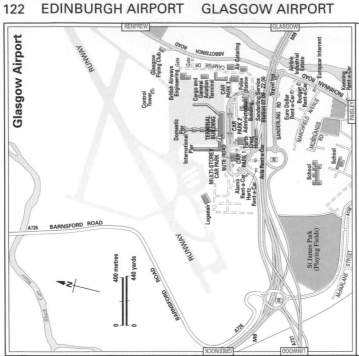

Glasgow Airport

RENFREW
GLASGOW
ABBOTSINCH ROAD
M8
CAMPSIE DR
Glasgow Flying Club
British Airways Engineering Gate
Gate
Air Catering
Airlink Industrial Estate
Europcar Interrent
Control Tower
Cargo and General Aviation Terminal
CAR PARK 3
Police Station
Sanderling Service Station 07.00 - 22.00
Travel Inn
Euro Dollar Rent-a-Car
Budget Rent-a-Car
Kenning Rent-a-Car
SANDERLING RD
MARCHFIELD AVENUE
INCHINNAN ROAD
PAISLEY
Domestic Pier
International Pier
TERMINAL BUILDING
CAR PARK 2
Airport Administration Building
Forte Crest Hotel
Hertz Rent-a-Car
Avis Rent-a-Car
MOSSLANDS RD
School
MULTI-STOREY CAR PARK
BUTE ROAD
CAR PARK 1
26
Alamo Rent-a-Car
School
A726 BARNSFORD ROAD
RUNWAY
BARNSFORD ROAD
A726
Loganair
MARRLANE STREET
St James Park (Playing Fields)
RUNWAY
GREENOCK
M8
A737
LINWOOD
Black Cart
White Cart
400 metres
440 yards
N

Glasgow Airport - 8 miles west of Glasgow

Telephone: 0141 887 1111
Parking: Short and Long-stay parking is available, mostly open air. For charge details tel: 0141 889 2751
Public Transport: Regular coach services operate between central Glasgow and Edinburgh
There are several 3-star hotels within easy reach of the airport and car hire facilities are available

Edinburgh Airport

EDINBURGH
A8
LENNYMUIR
Turnhouse Flying Club
TURNHOUSE ROAD
Cargo Terminal
RAF Turnhouse
Gate
RUNWAY
General Aviation Terminal
Gate
Scottish Airports Engineering Dept
Edinburgh Stalis Hotel
EASTFIELD ROAD
GLASGOW ROAD
Staff Car Park
JUBILEE ROAD
Coach Park
MAIN CAR PARK
Police Station
Security Gate
Alamo Rent-a-Car
Avis Rent-a-Car
Airport Junction
RUNWAY
River Almond
Gate
TERMINAL BUILDING
B.A.Engineering
1 HOUR CAR PARK Car hire return
Airport Administration Offices
Europcar Rent-a-Car
Hertz Rent-a-Car
FAIRVIEW ROAD
Port Royal Golf Range
Scottish Agricultural Museum
Euro Dollar Rent-a-Car
INGLISTON ROAD
Air Catering
Exhibition Hall
Royal Highland Showground (Ingliston)
Royal Highland Lodge (Hotel)
Parade Ring
R.H.A.S.S. Offices
Rural Centre
Sunday Market
A8
RUNWAY
GLASGOW
200 metres
220 yards
N

Edinburgh Airport - 7 miles west of Edinburgh

Telephone: 0131 333 1000
Parking: Open air parking is available. For charge details tel: 0131 344 3197
Public Transport: Regular coach services operate between central Edinburgh and Glasgow
There is one 4-star are several 3-star hotels within easy reach of the airport and car hire facilities are available

CHANNEL TUNNEL

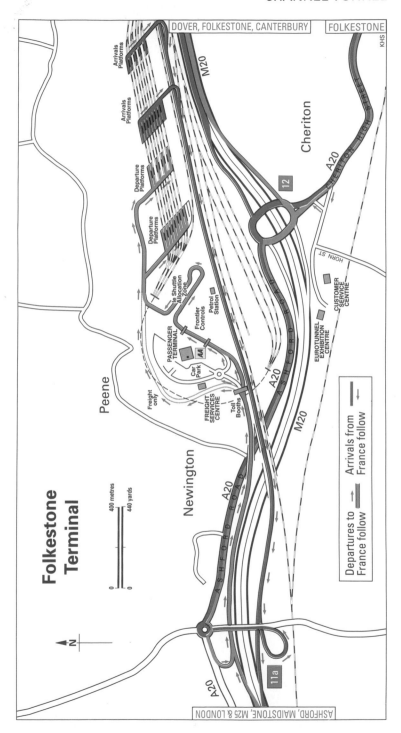

Folkestone Terminal

DOVER, FOLKESTONE, CANTERBURY

FOLKESTONE

KHS

Arrivals Platforms

Arrivals Platforms

Departure Platforms

Departure Platforms

M20

Cheriton

A20

12

CHERITON HIGH STREET

le Shuttle Allocation Zone

Frontier Controls

Petrol Station

PASSENGER TERMINAL

AA

Car Park

HORN ST

CUSTOMER SERVICE CENTRE

Freight only

FREIGHT SERVICES CENTRE

Toll Booths

EUROTUNNEL EXHIBITION CENTRE

A20

ASHFORD ROAD

M20

Peene

Newington

A20

ASHFORD ROAD

400 metres

440 yards

0

0

N

Departures to France follow

Arrivals from France follow

A20

11a

ASHFORD, MAIDSTONE, M25 & LONDON

Distance Chart

The distances between towns on the mileage chart are given to the nearest mile, and are measured along the normal AA recommended routes. It should be noted that AA recommended routes do not necessarily follow the shortest distances between places but are based on the quickest travelling time, making maximum use of motorways or dual-carriageway roads.

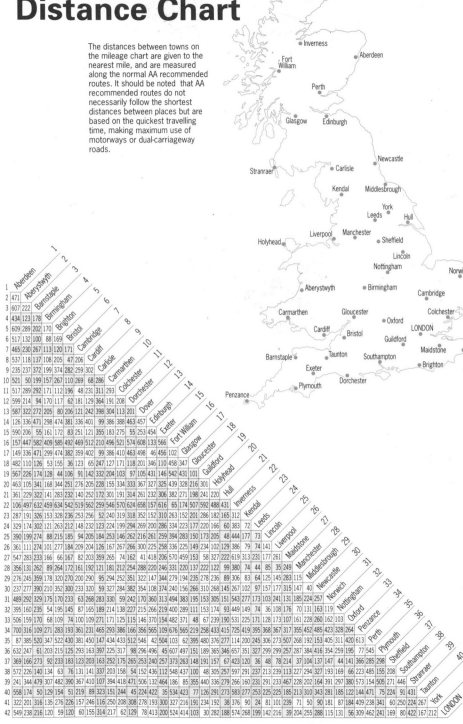

Places (numbered keys on the chart):

1 Aberdeen
2 Aberystwyth
3 Barnstaple
4 Birmingham
5 Brighton
6 Bristol
7 Cambridge
8 Cardiff
9 Carlisle
10 Carmarthen
11 Colchester
12 Dorchester
13 Dover
14 Edinburgh
15 Exeter
16 Fort William
17 Glasgow
18 Gloucester
19 Guildford
20 Holyhead
21 Hull
22 Inverness
23 Kendal
24 Leeds
25 Lincoln
26 Liverpool
27 Maidstone
28 Manchester
29 Middlesbrough
30 Newcastle
31 Norwich
32 Nottingham
33 Oxford
34 Penzance
35 Perth
36 Plymouth
37 Sheffield
38 Southampton
39 Stranraer
40 Taunton
41 York
42 LONDON

Mileage chart (distances in miles):

2 471
3 607 222
4 434 123 178
5 609 289 202 170
6 517 132 100 88 169
7 465 230 267 113 120 171
8 537 118 137 108 205 47 206
9 235 237 372 199 374 282 259 302
10 521 50 199 157 267 110 269 68 286
11 517 289 292 171 112 196 48 231 311 293
12 599 214 94 170 117 62 181 129 364 191 208
13 587 322 272 205 80 206 121 242 398 304 113 201
14 126 336 471 298 474 381 336 401 99 386 388 463 457
15 590 206 55 161 172 83 251 121 355 183 275 55 253 454
16 157 447 582 409 585 492 469 512 210 496 521 574 608 133 566
17 149 336 471 299 474 382 359 402 99 386 410 463 498 46 456 102
18 482 110 126 53 155 36 123 65 247 127 171 118 201 346 110 458 347
19 567 226 174 128 44 106 91 142 332 204 103 97 105 431 146 542 431 101
20 463 105 341 168 344 251 276 205 228 155 334 333 367 327 325 439 328 216 301
21 361 229 322 141 283 232 140 252 172 301 191 314 261 232 306 382 271 198 241 220
22 106 497 632 459 634 542 519 562 259 546 570 624 658 157 616 65 174 507 592 488 431
23 287 191 326 153 328 236 253 256 52 240 319 318 352 152 310 263 152 201 286 182 165 312
24 329 174 302 121 263 212 148 232 123 224 199 294 269 200 286 334 223 177 220 166 60 383 72
25 390 199 274 88 215 185 94 205 184 253 146 262 216 261 259 394 283 150 173 205 48 444 177 73
26 361 111 274 101 277 184 209 204 126 167 267 266 300 225 258 336 225 149 234 102 129 386 79 74 141
27 547 283 233 166 66 167 82 203 359 265 74 162 41 418 206 570 459 153 58 327 222 619 313 231 177 261
28 356 131 262 89 264 172 161 192 121 181 212 254 288 220 246 331 220 137 222 122 99 380 74 44 85 35 249
29 276 245 359 178 320 270 200 290 95 294 252 351 322 147 344 279 194 235 278 236 89 306 83 64 125 145 283 115
30 237 277 390 210 352 300 233 320 59 327 284 382 354 108 374 240 156 266 310 268 145 267 102 97 157 177 315 147 40
31 489 292 329 175 170 233 63 268 283 330 59 242 170 360 313 494 383 195 153 305 151 543 277 173 103 241 131 185 224 257
32 395 160 235 54 195 145 87 165 189 214 138 227 215 266 219 400 289 111 153 174 93 449 149 74 36 108 176 70 131 163 119
33 506 159 170 68 109 74 100 109 271 171 125 115 146 370 154 482 371 48 67 239 190 531 225 171 128 173 107 161 228 260 162 103
34 700 316 109 271 283 193 361 231 465 293 386 166 356 565 109 676 565 219 258 433 415 725 419 395 368 367 317 355 452 485 423 328 264
35 87 385 520 347 522 430 381 450 147 434 433 512 546 42 504 103 62 395 480 376 277 114 200 245 306 273 507 268 192 153 405 311 420 613
36 632 247 61 203 215 125 293 163 397 225 317 98 296 496 45 607 497 151 189 365 346 657 351 327 299 395 287 384 416 354 259 195 77 545
37 369 166 273 92 233 183 123 203 163 252 175 265 253 240 257 373 263 148 191 157 67 423 120 36 48 78 214 37 104 137 147 44 141 366 285 298
38 572 226 140 134 63 76 131 141 337 203 158 54 152 436 112 548 437 100 48 305 257 597 291 237 213 239 113 227 294 327 193 169 66 223 485 155 208
39 241 344 479 307 482 390 307 410 107 394 418 471 506 132 464 186 85 355 440 336 279 266 160 231 291 233 467 228 202 164 391 297 380 573 154 505 271 446
40 558 174 50 129 154 51 219 89 323 151 244 45 224 422 77 534 423 177 126 291 273 583 277 253 225 225 185 213 310 343 281 185 122 144 471 75 224 91 431
41 322 201 316 135 276 226 157 246 116 250 208 308 278 193 300 327 216 191 234 192 38 376 90 24 81 101 239 71 50 90 181 87 184 409 238 341 60 250 224 267
42 549 238 216 120 59 120 60 155 314 217 62 129 78 413 200 524 414 103 30 282 188 574 268 199 142 216 39 204 255 288 115 131 56 309 462 241 169 80 422 167 212